World Wisdom
The Library of Perennial Philosophy

The Library of Perennial Philosophy is dedicated to the exposition of the timeless Truth underlying the diverse religions. This Truth, often referred to as the *Sophia Perennis*—or Perennial Wisdom—finds its expression in the revealed Scriptures as well as the writings of the great sages and the artistic creations of the traditional worlds.

The Sufi Doctrine of Rūmī: Illustrated Edition appears as one of our selections in the Spiritual Masters: East & West series.

Spiritual Masters: East & West Series

This series presents the writings of great spiritual masters of the past and present from both East and West. Carefully selected essential writings of these sages are combined with biographical information, glossaries of technical terms, historical maps, and pictorial and photographic art in order to communicate a sense of their respective spiritual climates.

Page from a manuscript of Rūmī's *Mathnawī*

The Sufi Doctrine of
Rumi

Illustrated Edition

William C. Chittick

Foreword by
Seyyed Hossein Nasr

World Wisdom

The Sufi Doctrine of Rūmī: Illustrated Edition
© 2005 World Wisdom, Inc.

Book design by Susana Marín
Cover art: Persian miniature from Bukhārā, 16th century

Most recent printing indicated by last digit below
10 9 8 7 6 5 4 3 2

Library of Congress Cataloging-in-Publication Data

Chittick, William C.
  The Sufi doctrine of Rumi / William C. Chittick ; foreword by Seyyed Hossein Nasr.-- Illustrated ed.
    p. cm. -- (Spiritual masters. East and West series)
  Includes index.
  ISBN-10: 0-941532-88-7 (pbk. : alk. paper)
  ISBN-13: 978-0-941532-88-4 (pbk. : alk. paper)
  1. Jalāl al-Dīn Rūmī, Maulana, 1207-1273. 2. Sufism--Doctrines. I. Title. II. Series.
  BP189.7.M42C48 2005
  297.4'092--dc22
                                                    2005005943

Printed on acid-free paper in China.

For information address World Wisdom, Inc.
P.O. Box 2682, Bloomington, Indiana 47402-2682
www.worldwisdom.com

Contents

Calligraphy of the name of Rūmī

Foreword

Thanks to the translation of most of the works of Jalāl al-Dīn Rūmī into English from the eighteenth century to the present day by such scholars as Sir William Jones, E.H. Whinfield, J. Redhouse, and especially R.A. Nicholson and A.J. Arberry, followed in recent years by more popular American translations by Coleman Barks and others, this peerless Sufi poet and sage is now well known in the English-speaking world. He is in fact one of the most popular poets these days in America. But most of the studies devoted to him in Western languages have been concerned with literary and historical aspects of his works and only occasionally with an analysis of the symbolism of his language or the inner meaning of his tales and narratives. Rarely has there been a study of his metaphysical teachings in a succinct and penetrating manner.

It is true that Rūmī did not write direct metaphysical expositions as did an Ibn 'Arabī or Sadr al-Dīn Qunyawī. But Jalāl al-Dīn was a metaphysician of the first order and dealt with nearly every gnostic and metaphysical question, but often in the form of parables, narratives, or other forms of literary devices and poetic symbols. To understand his metaphysical doctrines, it is necessary to delve into the *Mathnawī* and the *Dīwān* as well as the *Fīhi mā fīhi* in depth and to extract those passages which bear directly upon metaphysics.

In this monograph William Chittick, who has already given us the wonderful *Sufi Path of Love* dealing with Rūmī, has succeeded in accomplishing such a task at least in so far as it concerns certain major aspects of traditional doctrines. The study of Dr. Chittick has the great merit, furthermore, of approaching the subject from a strictly traditional point of view untainted by the modernistic fallacies which have colored most of the other studies devoted so far to this subject in Western languages.

Some thirty years ago on the occasion of the seven hundredth year of the death of Jalāl al-Dīn Rūmī, Aryamehr University of Iran was proud to be able to participate in the international celebration devoted to this towering figure by making possible the original publication of this treatise. It is a testimony to the valuable nature of this early work of Dr. Chittick—who has since produced so many important works on Sufism—that this treatise is now being reprinted and made available in a beautiful new edition with illustrations to the lovers of Rūmī, who remains to this day a strong living influence in Persian and Turkish cultures and is now becoming a source of spiritual nourishment for seekers the world over. It is hoped that this and other studies which concern his ever-living spiritual and intellectual message will bring him ever more into the arena of contemporary life, where his teachings have the greatest relevance to the situation of modern man, faced as he is with the insoluble problems created by his own ignorance. May the message of Rūmī serve as a beacon of light to dispel the shadows which prevent modern man from seeing even his own image in its true form, and from knowing who he really is.

Seyyed Hossein Nasr
Former Chancellor, Aryamehr University, Iran
University Professor of Islamic Studies
The George Washington University
Dhu'l-Hijjah 1425
January 2005

The *samā'* or mystical dance of the dervishes

Preface to the Second Edition

This book was first published in 1974 by Aryamehr University in Tehran, where I was an assistant professor teaching Religious Studies. I had just finished a Ph.D. in Persian literature at Tehran University, having written a dissertation on 'Abd al-Rahmān Jāmī, a fifteenth century poet and a major commentator on Ibn 'Arabī. My interest in Rūmī, however, went back to my undergraduate years. I had spent most of my senior year in college (1965-66) writing a research paper on his teachings. I had no knowledge of Persian, but much of his poetry was already available in English because of the prodigious efforts of the great British orientalists, R. A. Nicholson and A. J. Arberry.

There were also a number of book-length studies available at that time, but it seemed to me that they largely missed the point. I was awfully young to be making such a judgment, but I trusted my instinct that a number of scholars—usually classified nowadays as "traditionalists" or "perennialists"—had made an authentic connection with Sufism's living lineage. In contrast, most of those known as "orientalists" seemed to have no real notion of what Sufism meant to its practitioners, nor did they take seriously the role of spirituality in human affairs. Thirty-eight years later, I cannot say that I was wrong. I still think that the traditionalist authors provide a door into the Sufi worldview that is not available through other sources.

I filed that undergraduate paper away for future reference, and then dusted it off and revised it thoroughly when Seyyed

Hossein Nasr, then chancellor of Aryamehr University, was looking for manuscripts to publish on the occasion of the celebration of the seven hundredth anniversary of Rūmī's death. Neither when I wrote the original, nor when I published the book, did I have any idea that Rūmī would soon become one of America's favorite poets. What I did understand was that he is the best English-language primary source for entrance into the rich symbolic world of Sufism. This is still probably the case. Nonetheless, despite the enormous popularity he has now gained, most people who read him do not have the necessary background to understand what he is getting at.

At the time I published the book, I thought it would be a useful tool for those who wanted to become familiar enough with Rūmī's worldview to make good use of the academic translations then available. Today the situation is quite different. Nicholson and Arberry remain relatively unread, but anthologies of Rūmī's poetry are common. Most of these have been put together by translators who in fact have little or no knowledge of the Persian language but who are adept at rephrasing the academic translations in attractive, contemporary English. These new translations have done a great service by catching some of Rūmī's magic and bringing him to the attention of an audience that otherwise would never have been exposed to him. What they generally fail to do, however, is to provide sufficient context to grasp what Rūmī is actually saying. For those who know him only through the popularizing translations, this little book may provide some insight into his universe of meaning.

Since this book first appeared, there has been a great upsurge not only in renditions of Rūmī's poetry, but also in scholarship.

Foremost among scholarly books is Annemarie Schimmel's *The Triumphal Sun* (1978), a masterly and thoroughly contextualized study of his literary contribution, concepts, and symbolism. Most recently we have Franklin Lewis' excellent survey of Rūmī's life, times, historical and religious context, and his literary influence down to the present, *Rumi: Past and Present, East and West* (2000). Lewis also provides a thorough bibliography and an evaluation of the scholarly and popular literature.

In 1983 I published a much longer study of Rūmī called *The Sufi Path of Love: The Spiritual Teachings of Rumi*. Lewis thinks that it is "an important advance in our knowledge of Rūmī's theosophy" (*Rumi*, p. 560). I had written *The Sufi Doctrine of Rūmī* attempting to bring out Rūmī's universal message in the context of Islamic spirituality, but in this new book I wanted to make full use of his own words and imagery to clarify the particularities and specificities of his approach.

Already in the Islamic world, from the fourteenth century onward, most of Rūmī's commentators relied heavily on Ibn 'Arabī's school of thought to provide structure to his writings, the same way that I do in *The Sufi Doctrine of Rūmī*. Down through the nineteenth century this school set the tone for most discussions of Sufism's theoretical framework. By the time I set out to write *The Sufi Path of Love*, I had studied everything Rūmī had written in the original languages, and it had become obvious to me that interpreting Rūmī in terms of Ibn 'Arabī is not completely fair to his perspective, though it is certainly preferable to methodologies not rooted in the tradition. I wanted to let him speak for himself. Unlike most Sufi poets, Rūmī explains the meaning of his imagery and symbolism. My task was simply to juxtapose various verses and prose passages to let him say what he wants to say.

In that second book on Rūmī, I used my own translations. When I published *The Sufi Doctrine of Rūmī* nine years earlier, I had seen no reason to attempt to improve on the translations of Nicholson and Arberry, since they were perfectly adequate for the points I wanted to make. When World Wisdom approached me about republishing the book, I was hesitant, not least because I would have preferred to use my own translations and perhaps revise a few of my interpretations. Thirty years, after all, is a long time, and the author of this book is in many ways a stranger to me. When I finally sat down and read the text from beginning to end for the first time since it was published, I was surprised to see that I agree with practically everything he has to say, though I myself would not say it in exactly the same way. Hence I left the text untouched, with the exception of typos and two or three footnotes that needed to be brought up to date.

William C. Chittick
Stony Brook University
26 November 2004

The oldest portrait of Mawlānā ("Our Master," i.e. Rūmī)

Introduction

Jalāl al-Dīn Rūmī, one of the greatest spiritual masters of Islam, is well known in the West and next to al-Ghazzālī perhaps the Sufi most studied by Western orientalists. A good portion of his writings have been translated into English, mainly through the efforts of the outstanding British orientalists R.A. Nicholson and A.J. Arberry.[1] But despite numerous studies of him, until now there has been no clear summary in English of the main points of his doctrines and teachings.[2] This lacuna has had the result that many Westerners wishing to be introduced to his thought are either overwhelmed by the great mass of his writing available in English, or, even if possessed of the patience to read through these works, unable

---

[1] Earlier scholars such as E. H. Whinfield, J. Redhouse, and C. E. Wilson had translated portions of the *Mathnawī*, but it is Nicholson's work which is a true milestone of orientalism. He edited and translated the whole of the *Mathnawī*, in six volumes, and in addition wrote two volumes of commentary, London, Luzac and Co., 1925-40. Arberry retranslated some of the stories from the *Mathnawī* as independent units (without Rūmī's continual didactic digressions) in *Tales from the Mathnawī*, London, 1963, and *More Tales from the Mathnawī*, London, 1968. Nicholson had earlier edited and translated a few poems from the *Dīwān*: *Selected Poems from the Dīvāni Shamsi Tabrīz*, Cambridge University Press, 1898, and Arberry continued this task, first in *The Rubā'īyāt of Jalāl ad-Dīn Rūmī*, London, 1949, and more recently in *Mystical Poems of Rūmī*, Chicago, 1968, a selection of 200 *ghazals*. Arberry also translated selections from one of Rūmī's prose works, *Fīhi mā fīhi*, as *Discourses of Rūmī*, London, John Murray, 1961.

The most important publications of the Persian texts of Rūmī's works include the following: the *Mathnawī* by Nicholson, as mentioned above, reprinted several times in Tehran; the *Dīwān*, critically edited by the late Badī' al-Zamān Furūzānfar in ten volumes, including a glossary and an index of verses, Tehran, 1336-46 (all Islamic dates are A.H. solar unless otherwise stated); *Fīhi mā fīhi*, edited by Furūzānfar, Tehran, 1330; and *Majālis-i sab'ah* ("Seven Gatherings") and *Maktūbāt* ("Letters"), both of which were edited by H. Ahmed Remzi Akyurek and published, in two volumes, by M. Nafiz Uzluk, Istanbul, 1937. The *Majālis-i sab'ah* was republished in the introduction of the edition of the *Mathnawī* edited by Muhammad Ramadānī, Tehran, Kulāla-yi Khāwar, reprinted, 1973. For a complete bibliography of the published texts of Rūmī's works, as well as translations and studies in all languages, see M. Sadiq Behzādi, *Bibliography of Mowlavi*, Tehran, 1973.

[2] In French there is the excellent recent study by E. Meyerovitch: *Mystique et poésie en Islam: Djalāl-ud-Dīn Rūmī et l'ordre des derviches tourneurs*, Paris, 1972. Among works in English which have attempted without much success to elucidate Rūmī's doctrine are Khalifa Abdul Hakim's *The Metaphysics of Rūmī*, Lahore, 1959 and Afzal Iqbal's *The Life and Thought of Rūmī*, Lahore, 1955, both of which hopelessly confuse the issue by referring to categories of modern Western philosophy which have no relevance to Rūmī. A.R. Arasteh's study, *Rūmī the Persian: Rebirth in Creativity and Love*, Lahore, 1965, contains some interesting material, particularly in showing how modern psychology fails to deal with the healthy and whole psyche. However, the author follows his personal opinion and the biases of psychoanalysis in dealing with Sufi doctrine and, like most modernized orientals, shows an astounding lack of both a sense of proportion and an understanding of the meaning of the sacred.

to form a clear picture of Rūmī's teachings because of his "unsystematic" method of exposition.

The present essay is an attempt to fill this gap and therefore to provide an introduction to Rūmī's doctrine which it is hoped will facilitate further study. This essay is not offered as a comprehensive analysis of Rūmī teachings, nor is there any attempt to exhaust their innumerable ramifications. To claim so would be a great presumption on my part, even were the subject of the study a lesser master than Rūmī, whose most well-known work, the *Mathnawī,* has often been called "the Quran in the Persian language."[3] For, like the Word of God revealed to the Arabian prophet, it contains within itself the essence of all knowledge and science (although it goes without saying on a lower level of inspiration). Even on the purely mundane and "academic" level it is a compendium of all of the Islamic sciences, from jurisprudence to astronomy.

My task, therefore, has been to present plainly and briefly the main points of Sufi doctrine as expounded in Rūmī's writings and at the same time to situate Sufism within Islam. Obviously, even were I qualified to deal with all the dimensions of these few points, a thorough study of them would require a work far beyond the scope of this essay. For this reason in many cases I have been able to do no more than make a brief allusion to the various problems which should be dealt with more extensively in a fuller study of Rūmī's thought. However, the relatively large number of authentic expositions of Sufi doctrine that have appeared in English over the past few years[4] enables me to limit myself to making reference to them where appropriate.

Rūmī's life and works have received much more competent attention in English than his teachings and there is nothing, therefore, that I can add to what has already been said.[5] However, for the benefit of some readers who may have no acquaintance with Mawlānā ("our Master," as he is commonly called in

[3] E. G. Browne among others has pointed this out, in *A Literary History of Persia*, 4 vols., London, 1902-24, vol. 2, p. 519.

[4] These include T. Burckhardt, *An Introduction to Sufi Doctrine*, Lahore, 1959; S.H. Nasr, *Three Muslim Sages*, Cambridge (Mass.), 1964, chapter 3; Nasr, *Ideals and Realities of Islam*, London, 1966; Nasr, *Sufi Essays*, London, 1972; M. Lings, *A Sufi Saint of the Twentieth Century*, London, 1971; and the works of F. Schuon, especially *Understanding Islam*, London, 1962 and *Dimensions of Islam*, London, 1969.

[5] See Browne, *A Literary History of Persia*; Iqbal, *Life and Thought of Rūmī*; the article "Djalāl al-Dīn Rūmī" in the new *Encyclopedia of Islam*; Nicholson, *Rūmī: Poet and Mystic*, London, 1950; and J. Rypka, *History of Iranian Literature*, Dordrecht, 1968, pp. 250-52. The most important material in Persian includes

Persian and Turkish), it may be useful to briefly summarize his life and the importance of his writings.

Jalāl al-Dīn Rūmī was born in Balkh in Khurasan on September 30, 1207, the son of Bahā' al-Dīn Walad, a man noted for his learning and himself a Sufi.[6] In 1219 Bahā' al-Dīn fled with his family from Balkh because of the impending invasion of the Mongols. After several years of wandering he finally settled in Konia in present-day Turkey, where he occupied a high religious office and was given the title "king of the religious scholars" (*sultān al-'ulamā'*). At the death of Bahā' al-Dīn in 1231, Jalāl al-Dīn succeeded him in his religious function, but it was not until after ten years of study that he could lay claim to being his father's true successor as a learned scholar held in high esteem by the Muslim community.

Following in his father's footsteps, Mawlānā became attracted to Sufism early in life and became the disciple of a number of spiritual masters. Perhaps the most important occurrence in his spiritual life was his meeting at the age of thirty-seven with a wandering Sufi named Shams al-Dīn of Tabriz.[7] The decisive change which subsequently overtook Rūmī is described by his son, Sultān Walad, as follows:

> *Never for a moment did he cease from listening to music and dancing:*
> *Never did he rest by day or night.*
> *He had been a* mufti: *he became a poet.*
> *He had been an ascetic: he became intoxicated by Love.*
> *'Twas not the wine of the grape: the illumined soul drinks only the wine of Light.*[8]

Aflākī's *Manāqib al-'ārifīn*, ed. by T. Yazici, 2 vols., Ankara, 1959-61, which had earlier been translated into French by C. Huart, *Les saints des derviches-tourneurs*, 2 vols., Paris, 1918; and the still fundamental study of Furūzānfar, *Risālah dar taḥqīq-i aḥwāl wa zindigī-yi Mawlānā Jalāl al-Dīn Muḥammad*, Tehran, 2nd ed., 1333 (1954). Also useful is E. Meyerovitch's study cited above, which in addition contains a good bibliography. S.H. Nasr's recent work, *Jalāl al-Dīn Rūmī: Supreme Persian Poet and Sage*, Tehran, 1974, is an excellent survey of Rūmī's life and works and the importance of his doctrine.

[6] Baha' Walad's *Ma'ārif* was edited in two volumes by Furūzānfar, Tehran, 1333-38.

[7] Shams' *Maqālāt* was recently published in a rather uncritical edition by A. Khwushniwīs, Tehran, 1349. Shams is an enigmatic figure in Sufism about whom little is known. S.H. Nasr has pointed out that Shams' role in Rūmī's life was to precipitate the remarkable flowering of spirituality and grace represented by the *Dīwān*, and that the extraordinary nature of Shams' personality is recognized symbolically by the Islamic community in the large number of tombs, all places of pilgrimage, which are attributed to him throughout the Islamic world (*Jalāl al-Dīn Rūmī*, pp. 22-23).

[8] Quoted by Nicholson, *Rūmī: Poet and Mystic*, p. 20.

For the remaining years of his life Rūmī was a Sufi who radiated the intoxication of Divine Love. In addition to writing (or rather, composing *extempore*) voluminously, he trained a large number of disciples, from whom was to stem the great Mevlevi order of Sufism. He died on December 16, 1273.

There has been unceasing praise for Rūmī's poetry ever since it was first set down in writing during his lifetime.[9] Western orientalists have called Rūmī "without doubt the most eminent Sufi poet whom Persia has produced,"[10] "the greatest mystical poet of Islam,"[11] and even "the greatest mystical poet of any age."[12] After translating the *Mathnawī*, Nicholson repeated this last statement, which he had first made thirty-five years earlier, for, he asked, "Where else shall we find such a panorama of universal existence unrolling itself through Time into Eternity?"[13]

The *Mathnawī*, a poem of 25,700 couplets, contains a great number of rambling stories and anecdotes of diverse style interspersed with digressions in which Rūmī usually explains the relevance of the stories to the spiritual life. The various sections of the *Mathnawī* seem to follow one another with no order, but in fact subtle links and transitions do lead from one theme to another. Moreover the symbolic and metaphoric method of presenting Sufi doctrine found in the *Mathnawī* is in many cases the best way for it to be imparted to aspirants on the spiritual path.[14] Rational analysis takes away much of the poetical magic and

[9] In Persia today Rūmī is still considered the greatest Sufi poet and has attracted a great deal of attention among contemporary scholars. His *Mathnawī* continues to play a major role in Persia's intellectual life. An indication of its importance is the number of commentaries upon it published within the last six or seven years. Among the most important of these are Furūzānfar's three volume work, Tehran, 1346-48, cut short at verse 3012 of the *Mathnawī*'s first book by the author's death; J. Humā'ī's commentary on the story of the "forbidden fortress" in the sixth book: *Tafsīr-i mathnawī-yi Mawlawī. Dāstān-i qal'ah-yi dhat al-suwar yā dizh-i hūsh-rubā*, Tehran, 1349; M. T. Ja'farī's *Tafsīr wa naqd wa tahlīl-i Mathnawī-yi Jalāl al-Dīn Balkhī*, Tehran, 1349 onward, of which eight volumes of over 500 pages each have appeared to date of a projected eighteen volumes; and the Persian translation by 'Ismat Sattār-zādah of Anqarawī's Turkish commentary: *Sharh-i kabīr-i Anqarawī bar Mathnawī*, Tehran, 1348 onward, of which four volumes have appeared, covering the first and second books.

[10] Browne, *A Literary History of Persia*, vol. 2, p. 515.

[11] Arberry, *Discourses*, p. ix.

[12] Nicholson, *Selected Poems*, preface.

[13] The *Mathnawī*, vol. 6, xiii.

[14] Persian Sufism very often followed this method, and many orders, such as the Ni'matullāhī, continue to do so to the present day. Listening to the words of a Sufi master, always interspersed with lines of poetry to carry home the points made, is a constant reminder that Sufi doctrine is first and foremost didactic, an aid on the spiritual Path, and not some philosophical system to be learned for its own sake.

"alchemical" power to transform the being of the listener and reduces the doctrine to cold philosophy.

Rūmī's second best known work is the *Dīwān-i Shams-i Tabrīz,* totaling some 40,000 couplets, which is a collection of poems describing the mystical states and expounding various points of Sufi doctrine. While the *Mathnawī* tends towards a didactic approach, the *Dīwān* is rather a collection of ecstatic utterances. It is well known that most of the *ghazals* (or "lyric poems of love") of the *Dīwān* were composed spontaneously by Mawlānā during the *samāʿ* or "mystical dance." This dance, which later came to be known as the "dance of the whirling dervishes," is an auxiliary means of spiritual concentration employed by the Mevlevi order, a means which, it is said, was originated by Rūmī himself.

A third work, *Fīhi mā fīhi* ("In it is what is in it"), translated by Arberry as *Discourses of Rūmī,* is a collection of Rūmī's sermons and conversations as recorded by some of his disciples.

It is my duty here to acknowledge my debt in all that I have learned concerning Sufism to Professor Seyyed Hossein Nasr, under whose direction I have had the honor to study for the past few years, and who, moreover, was kind enough to make numerous suggestions as to how the present essay could be improved. I am also indebted to Messrs. Jean-Claude Petitpierre and Lynn Bauman for their helpful suggestions. A preliminary version of the present study was written under Professor Harold B. Smith of the College of Wooster, Wooster, Ohio.

William C. Chittick
Aryamehr University, Tehran
December 8, 1973

I

Sufism and Islam

Page from a manuscript of Rūmī's *Mathnawī*

I. Sufism and Islam

Sufism is the most universal manifestation of the inner dimension of Islam; it is the way by which man transcends his own individual self and reaches God.[1] It provides within the forms of the Islamic revelation the means for an intense spiritual life directed towards the transformation of man's being and the attainment of the spiritual virtues; ultimately it leads to the vision of God. It is for this reason that many Sufis define Sufism by the saying of the Prophet of Islam concerning spiritual virtue (*ihsān*): "It is that thou shouldst worship God as if thou sawest Him, for if thou seest Him not, verily He seeth thee."

Islam is primarily a "way of knowledge,"[2] which means that its spiritual method, its way of bridging the illusory gap between man and God—"illusory," but none the less as real as man's own ego—is centered upon man's intelligence. Man is conceived of as a "theomorphic" being, a being created in the image of God, and therefore as possessing the three basic qualities of intelligence, free-will, and speech. Intelligence is central to the human state and gains a saving quality through its content, which in Islam is the *Shahādah* or "profession of faith": *Lā ilāha illallāh,* "There is no god but God"; through the *Shahādah* man comes to know the Absolute and the nature of reality, and thus also the way to salvation. The element of will, however, must also be taken into account, because it exists and only through it can man choose to conform to the Will of the Absolute. Speech, or communication with God, becomes the means—through prayer in general or in Sufism through quintessential prayer or invocation (*dhikr*)—of actualizing man's awareness of the Absolute and of leading intelligence and will back to their essence.[3]

---

[1] On the relationship between Sufism and Islam see S. H. Nasr, *Ideals and Realities of Islam*, chapter 5; Nasr, *Sufi Essays*, pp. 32 ff.; T. Burckhardt, *An Introduction to Sufi Doctrine*, chapter 1; and F. Schuon, *Understanding Islam*, chapters 1 and 4.

[2] See Schuon, *Understanding Islam*, pp. 13 ff. and Nasr, *Ideals and Realities*, pp. 21 ff.

[3] See Schuon, *Understanding Islam*, pp. 13 ff. and Nasr, *Ideals and Realities*, pp. 18 ff.

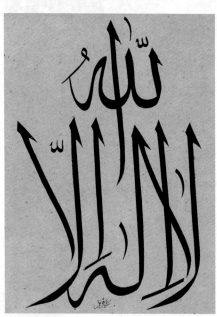

The *Shahādah* (calligraphy by Khurshid Alam)

Through the spiritual methods of Sufism the *Shahādah* is integrally realized within the being of the knower. The "knowledge" of Reality which results from this realization, however, must not be confused with knowledge as it is usually understood in everyday language, for this realized knowledge is "To know what is, and to know it in such a fashion as to be oneself, truly and effectively, what one knows."[4] If the human ego, with which fallen man usually identifies himself, were a closed system, such knowledge would be beyond man's reach. However, in the view of Sufism, like other traditional metaphysical doctrines, the ego is only a transient mode of man's true and transcendent self. Therefore the attainment of metaphysical knowledge in its true sense, or "spiritual realization," is the removal of the veils which separate man from God and from the full reality of his own true nature. It is the means of actualizing the full potentialities of the human state.

Metaphysical knowledge in the sense just described can perhaps be designated best by the term "gnosis" (*'irfān*), which in its original sense and as related to Sufism means "Wisdom made up of knowledge and sanctity."[5] Many Sufis speak of gnosis as being synonymous with love, but "love" in their vocabulary excludes the sentimental colorings usually associated with this term in current usage. The term love is employed by them because it indicates more clearly than any other word that in gnosis the whole of one's being "knows" the object and not just the mind; and because love is the most direct reflection in this world, or the truest "symbol" in the tradi-

[4] R. Guénon, "Oriental Metaphysics," *Tomorrow* (London), vol. 12, no. 1, p. 10; also in *The Sword of Gnosis*, Penguin Books, 1974.
[5] G.E.H. Palmer, in the foreword to Schuon, *Gnosis: Divine Wisdom*, London, 1959, p. 8.

tional sense, of the joy and beatitude of the spiritual world. Moreover, in Sufism, as in other traditions, the instrument of spiritual knowledge or gnosis is the heart, the center of man's being;[6] gnosis is "existential" rather than purely mental.

Rūmī indicates the profound nature of love (*'ishq* or *mahabbah*), a nature which can completely transform the human substance, by saying that in reality love is an attribute of God[7] and that through it man is freed from the limitations which define his state in the world.

> He (alone)[8] whose garment is rent by a (mighty) love is purged entirely of covetousness and defect.
> Hail, O Love that bringest us good gain—thou art the physician of all our ills,
> The remedy of our pride and vainglory, our Plato and our Galen (I, 22-24).

The interrelationship between love and knowledge is clearly expressed in the following passage:

> By love dregs become clear; by love pains become healing,
> By love the dead is made living....
> This love, moreover, is the result of knowledge: who (ever) sat in foolishness on such a throne?
> On what occasion did deficient knowledge give birth to this love? Deficient knowledge gives birth to love, but (only love) for that which is really lifeless (II, 1530-33).

In his commentary on these verses Nicholson recognizes that Rūmī does not differentiate between gnosis and love:

---

[6] On the heart, which is the seat of the Intellect in its traditional sense, see Schuon, "The Ternary Aspect of the Human Microcosm," in *Gnosis: Divine Wisdom*, chapter 7.

[7] See *Mathnawī*, V, 2185, where Rūmī states this explicitly. He also says, "Whether love be from this (earthly) side or from that (heavenly) side, in the end it leads us yonder" (I, 111). The sources of quotations from Rūmī are indicated as follows: Roman numerals refer to the particular volume of the *Mathnawī* (Nicholson's translation) being cited. *Discourses* refers to *Discourses of Rūmī*; *Dīwān* to *Selected Poems from the Dīvāni Shamsi Tabrīz*, and *Rubā'iyāt* to *The Rubā'iyāt of Jalāl al-Dīn Rūmī* (See Introduction, note 1).

[8] The additions within parentheses are Nicholson's; those within brackets are my own.

Rūmī ... does not make any ... distinctions between the gnostic (ʿārif) and the lover (ʿāshiq): for him, knowledge and love are inseparable and coequal aspects of the same reality.[9]

Rūmī describes the spiritual transformation brought about by love as follows:

> *This is Love: to fly heavenwards,*
> *To rend, every instant, a hundred veils* (Dīwān, p. 137).

> *Love is that flame which, when it blazes up, consumes everything else but the Beloved* (V, 588).

And therefore,

> *When love has no care for him [the traveler on the spiritual path], he is left as a bird without wings. Alas for him then! (I, 31).*

Sufism deals first and foremost with the inward aspects of that which is expressed outwardly or exoterically in the *Sharīʿah*, the Islamic religious law. Hence it is commonly called "Islamic esotericism."[10] In the view of the Sufis, exoteric Islam is concerned with laws and injunctions which direct human action and life in accordance with the divine Will, whereas Sufism concerns direct knowledge of God and realization—or literally, the "making real" and actual—of spiritual realities which exist both within the external form of the Revelation and in the being of the spiritual traveler (*sālik*). The *Sharīʿah* is directly related to Sufism inasmuch as it concerns itself with translating these same realities into laws which are adapted to the individual and social orders.

Exotericism by definition must be limited in some sense, for it addresses itself to a particular humanity and a particular

---

[9] *Mathnawī*, vol. VII, p. 294. In Sufism, contrary to Hinduism for example, there is no sharp distinction between the spiritual ways of love and knowledge; rather, it is a question of the predominance of one way over the other. See the excellent discussion by T. Burckhardt, "Knowledge and Love," in *Introduction to Sufi Doctrine*, pp. 27-32. On the various dimensions of love in Sufism as manifested in the world, see Schuon, "Earthly Concomitances of the Love of God," in *Dimensions of Islam*, chapter 9.

[10] On esotericism and exotericism, see Burckhardt, *An Introduction to Sufi Doctrine*, chapter 1; and Schuon, *The Transcendent Unity of Religions*, London, 1953, chapters 2 and 3.

psychological and mental condition—even though its means of addressing itself is to some degree universalized and expanded through time and space to encompass a large segment of the human race. Esotericism also addresses itself to particular psychological types, but it is open inwardly towards the Infinite in a much more direct manner than exotericism, since it is concerned primarily with overcoming all the limitations of the individual order. The very forms which somehow limit exotericism become for esotericism the point of departure towards the unlimited horizons of the spiritual world. Or again, exotericism concerns itself with forms of a sacred nature and has for its goal the salvation of the individual by means of these very forms, whereas esotericism is concerned with the spirit that dwells within sacred forms and has as its goal the transcending of all individual limits.

With these points in mind it should be clear why the Sufis acknowledge the absolute necessity of the *Sharī'ah* and in general are among its firmest supporters.[11] They recognize that to reach the indwelling spirit of a doctrine or a sacred form (such as a rite or a work of art), one must first *have* that external form, which is the expression of the Truth which that form manifests, but in modes conformable to the conditions of this world. Moreover, the vast majority of believers are not capable of reaching the inner meaning that lies within the revealed forms, and so they must attain salvation by conforming to the exoteric dimension of the revelation.

Here it may be helpful to quote from Ibn 'Arabī. This great Andalusian sage of the 7th/13th century (d. 1240) was the first to formulate explicitly many of the metaphysical and

---

[11] Sufism is also in a certain sense "opposed" to the *Sharī'ah*, although not in the way usually imagined. The spiritual Path is precisely a passing beyond or a penetrating into the forms of the *Sharī'ah*, and thus certain Sufis may at one time or another criticize the Divine Law, or rather those who follow it blindly, but only to warn them not to be limited and held back by it. The spiritual traveler must be able to pass to the inner essence of the Law, while at the same time following it on the individual and social planes. Deviations from Sufism have appeared when the Law has been ignored. On the equilibrium between esotericism and exotericism in Islamic civilization, see Nasr, *Ideals and Realities*, pp. 122 ff; and on a particular example during the Safavid period in Iran of opposition to Sufism caused by a rupture of this equilibrium, see Nasr, "Sūfism," *The Cambridge History of Iran*, vol. 4, edited by R. N. Frye, Cambridge, 1975, pp. 442-63.

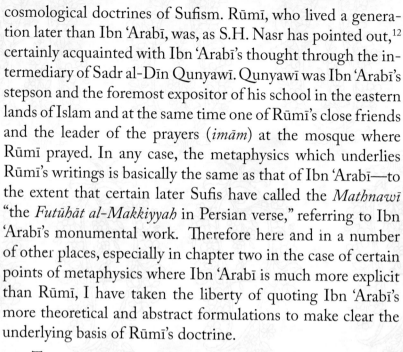

cosmological doctrines of Sufism. Rūmī, who lived a generation later than Ibn ʿArabī, was, as S.H. Nasr has pointed out,[12] certainly acquainted with Ibn ʿArabī's thought through the intermediary of Sadr al-Dīn Qunyawī. Qunyawī was Ibn ʿArabī's stepson and the foremost expositor of his school in the eastern lands of Islam and at the same time one of Rūmī's close friends and the leader of the prayers (*imām*) at the mosque where Rūmī prayed. In any case, the metaphysics which underlies Rūmī's writings is basically the same as that of Ibn ʿArabī—to the extent that certain later Sufis have called the *Mathnawī* "the *Futūḥāt al-Makkiyyah* in Persian verse," referring to Ibn ʿArabī's monumental work. Therefore here and in a number of other places, especially in chapter two in the case of certain points of metaphysics where Ibn ʿArabī is much more explicit than Rūmī, I have taken the liberty of quoting Ibn ʿArabī's more theoretical and abstract formulations to make clear the underlying basis of Rūmī's doctrine.

To return to the subject at hand, Ibn ʿArabī points out that traditions have their exoteric and esoteric sides in order that all believers may worship to their capacities.

> *The prophets spoke in the language of outward things and of the generality of men, for they had confidence in the understanding of him who had knowledge and the ears to hear. They took into account only the common people, because they knew the station of the People of Understanding.... They made allowances for those of weak intelligence and reasoning power, those who were dominated by passion and natural disposition.*
>
> *In the same way, the sciences which they brought were clothed in robes appropriate to the most inferior understandings, in order that he who had not the power of mystical penetration would stop at the robes and say, "How beautiful are they!", and consider them as the ultimate degree. But the person of subtle understanding who penetrates as one must into the depths after the pearls of wisdom will say, "These are robes from the King." He will contemplate the measure*

[12] "Rūmī and the Sufi Tradition," *Studies in Comparative Religion*, vol. 8, 1974, p. 79. On Ibn ʿArabī, see Nasr, *Three Muslim Sages*, Cambridge (Mass.), 1964, chapter 3.

14

*of the robes and the cloth they are made from and will come
to know the measure of Him who is clothed in the robes. He
will discover a knowledge which does not accrue to him who
knows nothing of these things.*[13]

In a similar vein Rūmī says the following:

*The perfect speaker is like one who distributes trays of
viands, and whose table is filled with every sort of food,*
*So that no guest remains without provisions, (but) each
one gets his (proper) nourishment separately:*
*(Such a speaker is) like the Quran which is sevenfold in
meaning, and in which there is food for the elect and for the
vulgar (III, 1895-97).*

Orientalists commonly speak of the derivation of Sufism
from non-Islamic sources and of its historical development.
From a certain point of view there has indeed been borrowing of forms of doctrinal expression from other traditions and
a great amount of development.[14] But to conclude from this

---

[13] Ibn ʿArabī, *Fusūs al-hikam*, edited by A. Afifi, Cairo, 1946, pp. 204-5.

[14] Orientalists have proposed a variety of theories as to the "origin" of Sufism, which
are well summarized in the introduction to R.A. Nicholson, *The Mystics of Islam*, London, 1914.

in the manner of many scholars that Sufism gradually came into being under the influence of a foreign tradition or from a hodgepodge of borrowed doctrine is to completely misunderstand its nature, i.e., that in essence it is a metaphysics and means of spiritual realization derived of necessity from the Islamic revelation itself.[15]

For the Sufis themselves one of the clearest proofs of the integrally Islamic nature of Sufism is that its practices are based on the model of the Prophet Muhammad. For Muslims it is self-evident that in Islam no one has been closer to God—or, if one prefers, no one has attained a more complete spiritual realization—than the Prophet himself, for by the very fact of his prophecy he is the Universal Man and the model for all sanctity in Islam. For the same reason he is the ideal whom all Sufis emulate and the founder of all that later became crystallized within the Sufi orders.[16]

According to Sufi teachings, the path of spiritual realization can only be undertaken and traversed under the guidance of a spiritual master; someone who has already traversed the stages of the Path to God and who has, moreover, been chosen by Heaven to lead others on the Way.[17] When the Prophet of Islam was alive he initiated many of his Companions into the spiritual life by transferring to them the "Muhammadan grace" (*al-barakat al-Muhammadiyyah*) and giving them theoretical and practical instructions not meant for all believers. Certain of these Companions were in their own turn given the function of initiating others.

---

[15] On the Islamic origin of Sufism, some of the proofs of which are briefly summarized here, see Nasr, *Ideals and Realities*, pp. 127 ff.; Nasr, *Sufi Essays*, pp. 16-17; and M. Lings, *A Sufi Saint of the Twentieth Century*, chapter 2.

[16] On the Sufi orders in their historical and social manifestation see J.S. Trimingham, *The Sufi Orders in Islam*, London, 1971.

[17] The absolute necessity for the spiritual master for entrance on the Sufi path is emphasized repeatedly in Rūmī's writings. On the significance of the master see Nasr, "The Sufi Master as Exemplified in Persian Sufi Literature," in *Sufi Essays*, chapter 4; and Schuon, "Nature and Function of the Spiritual Master," *Studies in Comparative Religion*, vol. 1, 1967, pp. 50-59.

The Sufi orders which came into being in later centuries stem from these Companions and later generations of disciples who received the particular instructions originally imparted by the Prophet. Without the chain (*silsilah*) of grace and practice reaching back to the Prophet no Sufi order can exist.

Gathering of Sufis

> *God's way is exceedingly fearful, blocked and full of snow. He [the Prophet] was the first to risk his life, driving his horse and pioneering the road. Whoever goes on this road, does so by his guidance and guarding. He discovered the road in the first place and set up waymarks everywhere* (Discourses, p. 232).

In the Sufi view of Islamic history, the very intensity of the spiritual life at the time of the Prophet did not permit a complete separation on the outward and formal plane between the exoteric and esoteric dimensions of the tradition. Both the *Shari'ah* and the *Tarīqah* (the spiritual path) existed from the beginning. But only after gradual degeneration and corruption—the tendency of the collectivity to become increasingly diversified and forgetful—was it necessary to make certain formulations explicit in order to refute the growing number of errors and to breathe new life into a decreasing power of spiritual intuition.[18]

---

[18] "According to a very prevalent error...all traditional symbols were originally understood in a purely literal sense, and symbolism properly so called only developed as the result of an 'intellectual progress' or a 'progressive refinement' which took place later. This is an opinion which completely reverses the normal relationship of things....In reality, what later appears as a super-added meaning was already implicitly present, and the 'intellectualization' of symbols is the result, not of an intellectual progress, but on the contrary of a loss by the majority of primordial intelligence. It is thus on account of increasingly defective understanding of symbols and in order to ward off the danger of 'idolatry' (and not to escape from a supposedly pre-existent, but in fact non-existent, idolatry) that the tradition has felt obliged to render verbally explicit symbols which at the origin...were in themselves fully adequate to transmit metaphysical truths." Schuon, "The Symbolist Outlook," *Tomorrow*, vol. 14, 1966, p. 50.

Rūmī was fully aware that on the collective level spiritual awareness and comprehension had dimmed since the time of the Prophet:

> *Amongst the Companions (of the Prophet) there was scarcely anyone that knew the Quran by heart [which is not such a rare accomplishment in the Islamic world today, whereas it must have been common at the time of Rūmī], though their souls had a great desire (to commit it to memory),*
>
> *Because … its kernel had filled (them) and had reached maturity (III, 1386–87).*

> *It is related that in the time of the Prophet … any of the Companions who knew by heart one Sura [chapter of the Quran] or half a Sura was called a great man … since they devoured the Quran. To devour a maund of bread or two maunds is certainly a great accomplishment. But people who put bread in their mouths without chewing it and spit it out again can "devour" thousands of tons in that way (Discourses, p. 94).*

If elaborated and systematized forms of Sufi doctrine were not present in early Islamic history, it is because such formulation was not necessary for the spiritual life. The synthetic and symbolic presentation of metaphysical truths found in the Quran and the *hadīth* (the sayings of the Prophet) was perfectly adequate to guide those practicing the disciplines of the *Tarīqah*. There was no need for detailed and explicit formulation. It was not until the third Islamic century/ninth Christian century in fact that the *Tarīqah* became clearly crystallized into a separate entity, at the same time that the *Sharī'ah* underwent a similar process.[19]

As for the similarities which exist between the formulation of Sufi doctrine and the doctrines of other traditions, in certain cases these *are* due to borrowings from other traditional sources. But here again it is a question of adopting a convenient mode of expression and not of emulating in-

---

[19] See Lings, *A Sufi Saint of the Twentieth Century*, pp. 42 ff.

ner spiritual states; in any case such states cannot be achieved through simple external borrowing. It would be absurd to suppose that a Sufi familiar with the doctrines of Neoplatonism, for example, who saw that the truths they expressed were excellent descriptions of his own inner states of realized knowledge, would completely reject the Neoplatonic formulations simply because of their source.[20]

In Sufism, doctrine has no right to exist "for its own sake," for it is essentially a guide on the Path. It is a symbolic prefiguration of the knowledge to be attained through spiritual travail, and since this knowledge is not of a purely rational order but is concerned ultimately with the vision of the Truth, which is Absolute and Infinite and in its essence beyond forms, it cannot be rigidly systematized. Indeed, there are certain aspects of Sufi doctrine which may be formulated by one Sufi in a manner quite different from, or even contradictory to, the formulations of another. It is even possible to find what appears outwardly as contradictions within the writings of a single Sufi. Such apparent contradictions, however, are only on the external and discursive level and represent so many different ways of viewing the same reality. There is never a contradiction of an essential order which would throw an ambiguity upon the nature of the transcendent Truth.

Doctrine is a key to open the door of gnosis and a guide to lead the traveler on the Path. Thus, for different people, different formulations may be used. Once the goal of the Path has been reached, doctrine is "discarded," for the Sufi in question *is* the doctrine in his inmost reality and he himself speaks with "the voice of the Truth."

> *After direct vision the intermediary is an inconvenience (IV, 2977).*

> *These indications of the way are for the traveler who at every moment becomes lost in the desert.*

---

[20] According to the famous saying of 'Alī, the representative *par excellence* of esotericism in Islam, "Look at what is said not at who has said it." Islamic civilization in general has always adopted any form of knowledge, provided it was in keeping with divine Unity (*tawḥīd*). See Nasr, *Ideals and Realities*, pp. 36 ff. and Nasr, *An Introduction to Islamic Cosmological Doctrines*, Cambridge (Mass.), 1964, p. 5.

For them that have attained (to union with God) there is nothing (necessary) except the eye (of the spirit) and the lamp (of intuitive faith): they have no concern with indications (to guide them) or with a road (to travel by).

If the man that is united (with God) has mentioned some indication, he has mentioned (it) in order that the dialecticians may understand (his meaning).

For a newborn child the father makes babbling sounds, though his intellect may make a survey of the (whole) world....

For the sake of teaching that tongue-tied (child), one must go outside of one's own language (customary manner of speech).

You must come into (adopt) his language, in order that he may learn knowledge and science from you.

All the people, then, are as his [the spiritual master's] children: this (fact) is necessary for the Pir [the master] (to bear in mind) when he gives (them) instruction (II, 3312 ff.).

In his preface to the fifth book of the *Mathnawī* Rūmī summarizes the relationship between the exoteric law (the *Sharī'ah*), the spiritual wayfaring which the Sufis undergo (the *Tarīqah*), and the Truth which is Sufism's goal (the *Haqīqah*). He says that the *Mathnawī* is:

...setting forth that the Religious Law is like a candle showing the way. Unless you gain possession of the candle, there is no wayfaring [i.e., unless you follow the Sharī'ah, *you cannot enter the* Tarīqah]; *and when you have come on to the way, your wayfaring is the Path; and when you have reached the journey's end, that is the Truth. Hence it has been said, "If the truths (realities) were manifest, the religious laws would be naught." As (for example), when copper becomes gold or was gold originally, it does not need the alchemy which is the Law, nor need it rub itself upon the philosopher's stone, which (operation) is the Path; (for), as has been said, it is unseemly to demand a guide after arrival at the goal, and blameworthy to discard the guide before arrival at the goal. In short, the Law is like learning the theory of alchemy from a teacher or book, and the Path is (like) making use*

of chemicals and rubbing the copper upon the philosopher's stone, and the Truth is (like) the transmutation of the copper into gold. Those who know alchemy rejoice in their knowledge of it, saying, "We know the theory of this (science)"; and those who practice it rejoice in their practice of it, saying, "We perform such works"; and those who have experienced the reality rejoice in the reality, saying, "We have become gold and are delivered from the theory and practice of alchemy: we are God's freedmen"....[21]

The law is [theoretical [22]] knowledge, the Path action, the Truth attainment unto God.

---

[21] On the spiritual significance of alchemy see T. Burckhardt, *Alchemy: Science of the Cosmos, Science of the Soul*, London, 1967.

[22] It should be remembered that the original meaning of the Greek word *theōria* is "viewing" or "contemplation"; doctrine is therefore "a view of the mountain to be climbed."

II

God and the World

"The Infinitude of the All-Possible"

Page from a manuscript of Rūmī's *Mathnawi*

II. God and the World
"The Infinitude of the All-Possible"[1]

The *Shahādah*, which epitomizes Islamic doctrine and hence also the doctrine of Sufism, may be said to contain two complementary perspectives, that of transcendence or incomparability (*tanzīh*) and that of immanence or resemblance (*tashbīh*). The first, transcendence, indicates that God is distinct from all beings and that absolutely nothing can compare to Him; the second, immanence, indicates that all beings derive their total reality from God and that therefore in their essential nature they have no reality outside of His Reality.[2]

"I bear witness that there is no god but God, He alone, without any partner."

If we substitute the Divine Name *al-Haqq*, which means at once "the Truth" and "the Real," for "God" in the *Shahādah*, the source of these two complementary points of view becomes apparent: "There is no real but the Real." On the one hand, God is the only reality in the absolute sense of the word, for to postulate that something else has autonomous reality

---

[1] "The infinitude of the All-Possible" is an expression borrowed from the writings of F. Schuon, who has expounded this traditional doctrine in remarkable fashion in several of his works, most recently in the article "*Ātmā-Māyā*," *Studies in Comparative Religion*, vol. 7, 1973, pp. 130-39.

[2] The complementary meanings of the *Shahādah* are explained with particular clarity by Schuon in *Understanding Islam*, pp. 16-18, 60-61, and 125-26.

vis-à-vis the Absolute Reality would involve polytheism or, in Islamic terms, "association" (*shirk*). Since God is the only real being, He is absolutely other than all created existence, which, if considered only in itself, is unreal. In the face of His absolute reality, all creatures are nothing. On the other hand, any reality that a creature does possess must ultimately belong to God. The Sufis would be the last to dispute the assertion that from a certain point of view (*i'tibār*) the world does indeed possess a certain limited reality, which, however, is not autonomous, but derives from that reality which in its absolute sense belongs to God alone.

As Ibn 'Arabī often points out in his *Fusūs al-hikam*,[3] the Quran summarizes these two points of view in the verse, "Nothing is like Him; and He is the Hearing, the Seeing" (XL, 9). There is nothing like God, so He is absolutely transcendent; but inasmuch as a being "hears" or "sees," it is from God that these attributes have come, or to be more exact, it is God who in reality is hearing and seeing. God is distinct from all created existence, but creation is not other than God in its essential nature.

Orientalists have often misrepresented Sufism by attempting to reduce such doctrines as the above to logical systems, or by isolating certain elements of the doctrine from their total context, saying, for example, that one Sufi contradicts another because the first asserts the transcendence of God while the second asserts His immanence. Actually, all true Sufis are perfectly aware of the double implication of the *Shahādah*, that God is both immanent and transcendent, or that, again in the words of Ibn 'Arabī,

> *If you profess transcendence (*tanzīh*), you delimit;*
> *If you profess immanence (*tashbīh*), you restrict.*
>
> *But if you profess both, you have been shown the right way:*
> *You are a leader in the gnostic sciences, a master.*[4]

---

[3] Ibn 'Arabī's exposition, very simply stated here, is explained in detail and great lucidity by T. Izutsu in his masterly study, *A Comparative Study of the Key Philosophical Concepts in Sufism and Taoism—Ibn 'Arabī and Lao-Tzu, Chuang-Tzu*, 2 volumes, Tokyo, 1966, vol. 1, pp. 49 ff.

[4] *Fusūs al-hikam*, p. 70.

If the emphasis of certain Sufis differs from that of other Sufis in this or other doctrines, it is because their expositions are aimed at guiding disciples on the spiritual path and not at explaining a philosophical system to orientalists.

One example of a common misrepresentation is to call certain Sufis "pantheists," Ibn 'Arabī being a prime target in this respect. It is true that both Sufism and pantheism say that the world is God, but Sufism adds immediately that God is absolutely other than the world, while classical pantheists say that the world is God with the implication that God is nothing but the sum total of the elements of the universe.[5]

It may be useful to repeat here that the prime reason certain scholars have misunderstood Sufi doctrine is that they do not see or cannot accept that its operative, or spiritually efficacious, elements are conceived of by the Sufis themselves as its only justification for existence. Such scholars are thus led to deal with Sufism as if it were another philosophical system capable of purely logical analysis, and in their attempts to delineate this "system" invariably misrepresent the doctrine. Moreover, in looking upon Sufi doctrine as only another kind of philosophy or mental construct, they often divorce it from its realized and "lived" dimen-

---

[5] "The exoteric mentality, with its one-sided logic and its somewhat passion-tainted 'rationality,' scarcely conceives that there are questions to which the answer is at once 'yes' and 'no'; it is always afraid of 'falling' into 'dualism,' 'pantheism,' 'quietism' or something of the kind. In metaphysics as in psychology it is sometimes necessary to resort to ambiguous answers; for example, to the question: the world, 'is it' God? we reply: 'no,' if by the 'world' is understood ontological manifestation as such, that is to say in its aspect of existential or demiurgic relativity; 'yes,' if by 'world' is understood manifestation in so far as it is causally or substantially divine, since nothing can be outside of God; in the first case, God is exclusive and transcendent Principle, and in the second, total Reality or universal and inclusive Substance. God alone 'is'; the world is a limited 'divine aspect,' for it cannot—if we are to avoid absurdity—be a nothingness on its own level. To affirm on the one hand that the world has no 'divine quality,' and on the other that it is real apart from God and that it never ceases so to be, amounts to admitting two Divinities, two Realities, two Absolutes." Schuon, *Gnosis: Divine Wisdom*, pp. 80-81. For a clear discussion of the reasons why the term "pantheism" does not apply to Sufism, see Burckhardt, *Introduction to Sufi Doctrine*, chapter 3.

sion. Only a misunderstanding of this sort could have led one orientalist to declare that Ibn ʿArabī was responsible for a "divorce of mystical thought and moral feeling" so that his doctrine was "religiously flat, sterile, and stultifying on later religion."[6] This statement is absurd unless we are to reduce religion to an empty moralism and say that God cannot be approached through the intelligence. The above criticism, moreover, is answered by Ibn ʿArabī in a passage which is a summary of the reason for the existence of traditional metaphysics:

> *The world is illusory: it has no real existence. This is what is meant by "imagination" (*khayāl*). You have been made to imagine that the world is something separate and independently real, outside of the Absolute. But in reality it is not so. Do you not see that in the world of sensory things a shadow is attached to the person from whom it originates and that it is impossible to separate a thing from its essence? Therefore know thy own essence and who thou art, what thy inmost nature is and what thy relation is to the Absolute. Know in what respect thou art the Absolute, in what respect the world, and in what respect "other" (than God), "different," etc. And here it is that "knowers" become ranked according to degrees.*[7]

Such knowledge, however, does not come from philosophical investigation; rather, it is the fruit of spiritual travail and metaphysical realization. It is simple to say that "God is real and the world is unreal," but it is something quite differ-

---

[6] W. Thompson, "The Ascetical-Mystical Movement and Islam," *Muslim World*, vol. 39, 1949, p. 282.

[7] *Fusūs al-hikam*, p. 103; also translated by Izutsu, *Comparative Study*, pp. 88-89.

ent to know this in an effective way, such that one's very being reflects this unitive knowledge. In Rūmī's words, "To know the science of "I am God"[8] is the science of bodies; to become "I am God" is the science of religions" (*Discourses*, p. 935).

According to Rūmī, the real nature of the relationship between God and the world is accessible only to gnosis. It cannot be known through rational processes and discursive thought.

> *No created being is unconnected with Him: [but] that connection, O uncle, is indescribable.*
>
> *Because in the spirit there is no separating and uniting, while (our) thought cannot think except of separating and uniting (IV, 3695-96).*

Nevertheless, in certain contexts Rūmī often offers analogies in the attempt to describe the relationship to the extent possible in human language. For example, he says of the Divine Being in its self-manifesting (*mutajallī*) aspect,

> *It ... is neither inside of this world nor outside; neither beneath it nor above it; neither joined with it nor separate from it: it is devoid of quality and relation. At every moment thousands of signs and types are displayed by it (in this world). As manual skill to the form of the hand, or glances of the eye to the form of the eye, or eloquence of the tongue to the form of the tongue, (such is the relation of that world to this) (V, p. 167).*

In Sufi doctrine the creation of the world is usually depicted as the manifestation of the attributes of God in the manner expressed by the famous *hadīth qudsī*[9]: "I was a hidden treasure and I wanted to be known, so I created the world." Rūmī refers to this *hadīth* often, as for example in the *Dīwān*, where he renders it poetically as follows:

---

[8] This well known "ecstatic utterance" for which al-Hallāj was put to death compares to others in Islamic history such as the "Glory be to me" of Bāyazīd al-Bastāmī and on another level to the saying of the Prophet, "He who has seen me has seen the Truth."
[9] A *hadīth qudsī* or "sacred tradition" is a saying of the Prophet in which God speaks through him in the first person.

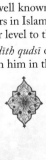

David said: "O Lord, since thou hast no need of us,
Say, then, what wisdom was there in creating the two
worlds?"

God said to him: "O temporal man, I was a hidden trea-
sure;

I sought that that treasure of lovingkindness and bounty
should be revealed…" (Dīwān, p. 15).

The celestial map of the macrocosm

Obviously, God knew Himself "before"[10] the creation of
the world, so what this *hadīth* expresses is that God wanted to
be known by "others," even though, as we have seen, "other than
God" has only an illusory and relative existence. God wanted
to be known in the distinctive and relative mode of knowledge
proper to created beings.[11] According to Ibn ʿArabī:

[10] "Before" is meant in a logical rather than temporal sense, because for God all manifestation exists in perfect simultaneity in the "eternal present." Temporal succession
exists only from a certain relative point of view. "'With God is neither morn nor eve':
there the past and the future and time without beginning and time without end do not
exist: Adam is not prior nor is Dajjāl (Antichrist) posterior. (All) these terms belong
to the domain of the particular (discursive) reason and the animal soul: they are not
(applicable) in the non-spatial and non-temporal world" (VI, p. 408).

[11] Schuon, *Light on the Ancient Worlds*, London, 1965, p. 89.

> *Nothing remained but the perfection of the dimension of Knowledge by contingent knowledge, which would derive from these concrete things—that is, the concrete things of the world—when actualized in external existence. In this manner there would appear the perfection of contingent knowledge and the perfection of eternal knowledge, and the dimension of Knowledge would reach perfection through these two aspects.*[12]

The possibility that God should determine Himself, or should make Himself known in a differentiated and distinctive mode, is necessitated by the Divine Infinity: since God is infinite, all possibilities of manifestation or "theophany" (*tajallī*) are open to Him. In the words of Frithjof Schuon, "The infinitude of Reality implies the possibility of its own negation,"[13] and this "negation of God" is precisely the created world: it "negates" Him because it limits His Reality to practically nothing by imposing upon it the limitations of form. Rūmī expresses this as follows: "That Reality, *qua* Reality, has no opposite, only *qua* form" (*Discourses*, p. 92). The world is "opposite" because it limits God by its form, yet it is nevertheless His Reality, the only Reality there is.

God in His self-manifestation (*tajallī*) makes Himself known at various levels of reality, levels which have been described in a variety of ways by different Sufis. According to one formulation, which pertains mainly to the school of Ibn ʿArabī, God "before" creation or before His own self-manifestation is conceived of as the Essence (*al-dhāt*), the absolutely unconditioned Reality. At this stage He is beyond all description, but we cannot even say this about Him, for to do so is in a sense to describe Him.

In becoming known, the "Hidden Treasure" or the unconditioned Reality of God gradually becomes determined and conditioned. The first determination (*al-taʿayyun al-awwal*) is referred to as *al-ahadiyyah*, the indivisible Unity. In it the divine Names and Qualities (*al-asmāʾ waʾl-sifāt*) are contained

---

[12] *Fusūs al-hikam*, p. 204; also translated by Izutsu, *Comparative Study*, pp. 131-32.
[13] *Gnosis: Divine Wisdom*, p. 72.

33

such that each is identified with and indistinguishable from every other. *Al-ahadiyyah* can only be the object of immediate and undifferentiated divine knowledge, not of any knowledge of an analytical or discursive order.

The second determination of the Essence is *al-wāhidiyyah*, or Unicity, in which the Names and Qualities are discernible such that each is distinct from every other. Strictly speaking, the manifested universe does not "begin" until below the level of Unicity, but it is convenient to speak of manifestation as everything which is other than the Essence.[14]

Each of the Divine Qualities contained in *al-wāhidiyyah* is unique, and each refers to a universal aspect of God which becomes manifest in the world. The indefinite multiplicity of the Qualities and their endless combinations determine on a lower level the *a'yān al-thābitah*, the immutable essences, archetypes, or principial possibilities of existent things. These in turn determine immutably each aspect of manifestation or creation, which from this point of view is thus a possibility subsisting eternally within the Divine Knowledge. The archetypes as such are never brought into existence in the sense of separate or externalized realities. They are not distinct substances, but rather possibilities of determination inherent in the Divine.

Just as the Essence is transcendent in regard to all manifestation, so each self-determination of the Essence, or each level of reality, is unaffected by those levels below it, although each contains the principles of the lower levels within itself and determines these levels absolutely. The levels below *al-wāhidiyyah* are beyond number but can be summarized into general categories: 1. *al-jabarūt*, the world of the archetypes or of spiritual existence; 2. *al-malakūt*, the worlds of psychic substances; 3. *al-nāsūt*, the worlds of material forms.

The concept of the levels of reality helps explain another basic Sufi doctrine, the renewal of creation at each instant.[15] At the level of *al-ahadiyyah*, all possibilities are present simultaneously, and only at the level of *al-wāhidiyyah* do they become separate and distinct. In the world of spiritual existence, *al-jabarūt*, each possibility will have a variety of reflections appearing as a richness of its indefinite aspects, each aspect containing in itself every other. In the lowest worlds, the cosmic condition of form must be taken into account, with the result that this richness becomes "spelled out" by the separate crystallizations of its numerous dimensions. Moreover, the different crystallizations of a divine possibility as they are manifested in one existent being in the world will appear successively, or temporally, precisely because the condition of form does not allow them to be revealed simultaneously. This is all the more so since the being always reflects the Oneness of

---

[15] On the concept of continuous creation see the extremely lucid study of T. Izutsu: "The Concept of Perpetual Creation in Islamic Mysticism and Zen Buddhism," in S.H. Nasr (ed.), *Mélanges offerts à Henry Corbin, herméneute de la tradition intellectuelle et spirituelle de l'Iran*, Tehran, 1974.

God, or the Divine Uniqueness, at every point in its manifestation. "Every instant," says Rūmī,

> thou art dying and returning [to existence]....
>
> Every moment the world is renewed, and we are unaware of its being renewed whilst it remains (the same in appearance).
>
> Life is ever arising anew, like the stream, though in the body it has the semblance of continuity (I, 1142 ff.).

The Quranic verse, "All is perishing but His face [Essence]" (XXVIII, 88), besides containing other levels of meaning, is an epitome of this doctrine of continual creation, a doctrine which emphasizes the ephemerality of the world and its absolute dependence upon its divine Source at every moment. Everything in the world, or rather "everything other than God" (*mā siwa'-llāh*), only exists to perish immediately.

> The world subsists on a phantom. You call this world real, because it can be seen and felt, whilst you call phantom those verities whereof this world is but an offshoot. The facts are the reverse. This world is the phantom world, for that Verity produces a hundred such worlds, and they rot and corrupt and become naught, and it produces a new world and better. That grows not old, being exempt from newness and oldness. Its offshoots are qualified by newness and oldness, but He who produces these is exempt from both attributes and transcends both (Discourses, p. 131).

The world for all its ephemerality and unreality must nevertheless exist on its own level. Ibn ʿArabī explains this in the following terms:

> *You are to Him as the corporeal body is to you, and He is to you as is the Spirit which governs your body. The definition of you includes your outward and your inward dimensions, for the body which is left behind when the governing spirit departs from it does not remain a human being; rather, it is said of it that it is the external form of a man, and there is no difference [in respect of its being a form] between it and the form of a piece of wood or a stone. The name "man" is applied to it only figuratively, not in the true sense of the word. But it is impossible that the Absolute could ever depart from the phenomenal forms of the world. Therefore the definition of "divinity" belongs to the world in the true sense, not figuratively, just as [the definition of man belongs to him] when the being is alive.*[16]

> *If from the Divine Essence were abstracted all the relations (i.e. the Names and Attributes), it would not be a God (*ilāh*). But what actualizes these (possible) relations (which are recognizable in the Essence) is ourselves. In this sense it is we who, with our own inner dependence upon the Absolute as God, turn it into a "God."*[17] *So the Absolute cannot be known until we ourselves become known.*[18]

The important point to note in the above passages is that creation must exist because of God's infinity. He can not *not* create the world. The very term "God," which in Arabic as employed by Ibn ʿArabī contains in itself the notion of reciproc-

---

[16] *Fuṣūṣ al-hikam*, p. 69; also partially translated by Izutsu, *Comparative Study*, p. 67.

[17] What is meant here is God as creator and sustainer of the universe. In Ibn ʿArabī's doctrine the name Allāh (and also the term *ilāh*) refers to the level of the Divine Names and Qualities, and therefore, to say "Allāh" is to imply the Divine Names such as *khāliq* (Creator), many of which by definition require a corresponding or reciprocal term, in this case *makhlūq* ("created"). The Absolute in its Essence, therefore, usually referred to by Ibn ʿArabī as *al-haqq*, cannot be called "God" in this sense, for, as pointed out above, the Essence is beyond all determinations. See Izutsu, *Comparative Study*, p. 17.

[18] *Fuṣūṣ al-hikam*, translated by Izutsu, *Comparative Study*, p. 34, with minor alterations by myself.

A king listens to the teachings of a Sufi

ity, would have no meaning if it were not for the dependence of creation upon Him. Creation is the "object" of His divinity (*maʿlūh*), or that in respect to which God is God. In the words of Rūmī,

> *When you say that this is a branch of that, until the branch exists how does the term "root" become applicable to the other? So it became root out of this branch; if the branch had not existed, it [the root] would never have had a name. When you speak of woman, there must necessarily be man; when you speak of Master, there must be one mastered; when you speak of Ruler, there must be one ruled* (Discourses, *p. 153*).

Since the world is the self-manifestation of God, what appears as evil and suffering in this world can in the last analysis be traced back to the Origin of creation Itself:

> *Do you not see that the Absolute appears in the attributes of contingent beings and thus gives knowledge about Himself; and that He appears in the attributes of imperfection and blame?*[19]

Hence, to ask why evil exists in the world is the same as to ask why there is a creation, and the answer is the infinity of God in His self-manifestation. Rūmī expresses this by comparing God to an artist who paints beautiful as well as ugly pictures:

> *Both kinds of pictures are (evidences of) his mastery....*
> *He makes the ugly of extreme ugliness—it is invested with all (possible) ugliness—*
> *In order that the perfection of his skill may be displayed, (and that) the denier of his mastery may be put to shame.*
> *And if he cannot make the ugly, he is deficient (in skill)...* (II, 2539 ff.).

---

[19] *Fusūs al-hikam*, p. 80; also translated by Izutsu, *Comparative Study*, p. 224.

Rūmī deals with the question of evil from a slightly different angle in a story about a man who asked a Sufi master the following question:

> *He (God) whose help is invoked hath the power to make our trading free from loss....*
> *He ... hath the power if He would turn sorrow into joy.*
> *He by whom every non-existence is made existent —what damage would He suffer if He were to preserve it (the world) forever?*
> *He who gives the body a soul that it may live— how would He be a loser if He did not cause it to die? (VI, 1739 ff.).*

The question is answered in two parts: first creation is necessarily differentiated into various qualities and attributes, including joy and sorrow and good and evil, because of the infinity of the Divine Nature, and because, in becoming "other than God," manifestation necessarily takes on particularized and opposing forms.

> *Were there no bitter (stern) Commandments (from God) and were there no good and evil and pebbles and pearls,*
> *And were there no flesh and Devil and passion, and were there no blows and battles and war,*
> *Then by what name and title would the King call His servants? (VI, 1747-49).*

Second even the cruelty of the world is in fact a Divine Mercy, for,

> *The cruelty of Time (Fortune) and every affliction that exists are lighter than farness from God and forgetfulness (of Him).*
> *Because these (afflictions) will pass, (but) that (forgetfulness) will not. (Only) he that brings his spirit (to God) awake (and mindful of Him) is possessed of felicity (VI, 1756-57).*

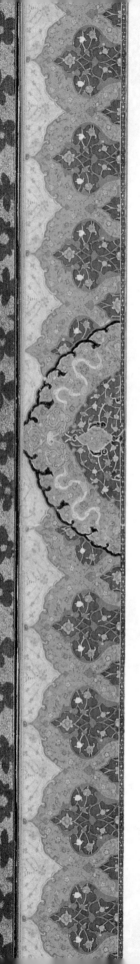

Thus man should be thankful that the world is full of evil and affliction, for these turn him toward God. So do not ask why creation is evil, and

> *Do not regard the (anxious) husbanding of (one's) daily bread and livelihood and this dearth (of food) and fear and trembling.*
> *(But) consider that in spite of all its (the World's) bitternesses ye are mortally enamored of it and recklessly devoted to it.*
> *Deem bitter tribulation to be a (Divine) mercy (VI, 1734-36).*

"From the point of view of God," all creation is performing but one task (*Discourses*, p. 221), i.e., that of revealing the "Hidden Treasure"; thus, by the very fact that a being exists, whether it does good or evil, it is worshipping God:

> *(All) our movement (action) is really a continual profession of faith which bears witness to the Eternal Almighty One (V, 3316).*

> *...(both) infidelity and faith are bearing witness (to Him): both are bowing down in worship before His Lordliness (II, 2534).*

> *Infidelity is ever giving praise to the Truth.*[20]

Such statements, of course, do not mean that Sufis advocate infidelity. Man is privileged among beings in that he has intelligence and free-will and therefore can disobey the commandments of God as well as obey them. "Man rides on the steed of 'We have honored (the sons of Adam)' [Quran, XVII, 72]: the reins of free-will are in the hand of his intelligence" (III, 3300). If he disobeys God's commands as set down by the prophets, he is revealing certain aspects of God but he is wronging himself, for although "all things in relation to God are good and perfect, ...in relation to us it is not so" (*Discourses*, p. 42). "God most High wills both good and

---

[20] Mahmūd Shabistarī, *Gulshan-i Rāz, the Mystic Rose Garden*, translated by E.H. Whinfield, London, 1880, verse 879. Shabistarī's *Gulshan-i Rāz* is a summary of the doctrines of Ibn ʿArabī and is one of the most important Sufi works in Persian.

The dance of
the dervishes

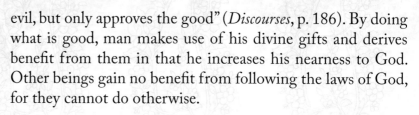

evil, but only approves the good" (*Discourses*, p. 186). By doing what is good, man makes use of his divine gifts and derives benefit from them in that he increases his nearness to God. Other beings gain no benefit from following the laws of God, for they cannot do otherwise.

> *Choice (free-will) is the salt of devotion; otherwise (there would be no merit): this celestial sphere revolves involuntarily;*
>
> *(Hence) its revolution has neither reward nor punishment....*
>
> *All created beings indeed are glorifiers (of God), (but) that compulsory glorification is not wage-earning (III, 3287-89).*

Miniature illustrating a story about Mawlānā and his candle, which is the spirit of all candles

III

The Nature of Man

Page from a manuscript of Rūmī's *Mathnawī*

III. The Nature of Man

1. Universal Man

Although the universe is one when seen from the point of view of the Divine Essence, from the point of view of relativity there is a fundamental polarization into microcosm and macrocosm. The macrocosm is the universe in all its indefinite multiplicity, reflecting the Divine Names and Qualities as so many individual particularizations and determined modes. The microcosm is man, who reflects these same qualities but as a totality. The macrocosm and the microcosm are like two mirrors facing each other; each contains all of the other's qualities, but the one in a more outward and objective manner and in detail (*mufassal*) and the other in a more inward and subjective manner and in summary form (*mujmal*). Thus man's total knowledge of himself in principle includes the knowledge of the whole universe. For this reason the Quran says, "And He [God] taught Adam the Names [i.e., the essences of all beings and things]" (II, 31).

> *The father of mankind, who is the lord of "He taught the Names," hath hundreds of thousands of sciences in every vein.*
>
> *To his soul accrued (knowledge of) the name of every thing, even as that thing exists (in its real nature) unto the end (of the world)....*
>
> *With us [ordinary men], the name of every thing is its outward (appearance); with the Creator, the name of every thing is its inward (reality)....*
>
> *Inasmuch as the eye of Adam saw by means of the Pure Light, the soul and inmost sense of the names became evident to him (I, 1234–35, 1239, 1246).*

The prototype of both the microcosm and the macrocosm is the Universal or Perfect Man (*al-insān al-kāmil*),[1] who is

---

[1] On the macrocosm and the microcosm and Universal Man see Burckhardt, *Introduction to Sufi Doctrine*, pp. 89 ff.; Izutsu, *Comparative Study*, chapters 14-17; and R. Guénon, *Symbolism of the Cross*, London, 1958. The title of Guénon's work is explained

the sum total of all levels of reality in a permanent synthesis. All the Divine Qualities are contained within him and integrated together in such a way that they are neither confused nor separated, and yet he transcends all particular and determined modes of existence. Moreover, in terms of revelation, Universal Man is the Spirit, of which the prophets are so many aspects, and of which from the Islamic point of view Muhammad is the perfect synthesis.

Universal Man has another aspect when seen from the point of view of the spiritual path: he is the perfect human model who has attained all of the possibilities inherent in the human state. In him the "Names" or essences which man contains in potentiality (*bi'l-quwwah*) are actualized so that they become the very states of his being (*bi'l-fi'l*). For him the human ego with which most men identify themselves is no more than his outer shell, while all other states of existence belong to him internally; his inward reality is identified with the inward reality of the whole universe.[2]

Universal Man is the principle of all manifestation and thus the prototype of the microcosm and the macrocosm. Individual man, or man as we usually understand the term, is the most complete and central reflection of the reality of Universal Man in the manifested universe, and thus he appears as the final being to enter the arena of creation, for what is first in the principial order is last in the manifested order.[3]

The term "Universal Man" was given prominence by Ibn 'Arabī, though the doctrine was well known before him, and necessarily so, for from the point of view of Sufism the Prophet of Islam is the most perfect manifestation of Universal Man.

by him as follows: "Most traditional doctrines symbolize the realization of 'Universal Man' by…the sign of the cross, which clearly represents the manner of achievement of this realization by the perfect communion of all the states of the being, harmoniously and conformably ranked, in integral expansion, in the double sense of 'amplitude' and 'exaltation.'" p. 10.

[2] Burckhardt, *Introduction to Sufi Doctrine*, p. 93; see also Guénon, *Symbolism of the Cross*, chapters 2 and 3.

[3] The Arabic dictum is *awwal al-fikr ākhir al-'amal*, "The first in thought is the last in actualization." The metaphysical principle is explained by Guénon in *Symbolism of the Cross*, p. 7. See also S.M. Stern, "'The First in Thought is the Last in Action': the History of a Saying Attributed to Aristotle," *Journal of Semitic Studies*, vol. 7, 1962, pp. 234-52.

It is essentially to this state that the Prophet was referring when he said, "The first thing created by God was my light (*nūrī*)" or "my spirit (*rūhī*)"—a *hadīth* which has been cited by Sufis over and over again throughout the centuries. Moreover, because numerous saints from the time of the Prophet onward reached this state, they knew the meaning of the doctrine of Universal Man in a concrete manner, even if they did not speak of it in exactly the same terms as did Ibn 'Arabī.

Before Ibn 'Arabī Universal Man was usually spoken of in slightly different terms from those employed by him: the "microcosm" in this earlier perspective is man's external form, while the "macrocosm" is his inward reality. In other words, the term "macrocosm" refers essentially to the inward reality of the Universe and not to its outward form, as is usually the case in Ibn 'Arabī's doctrine. But this inward reality is precisely Universal Man and is therefore identical with the inward reality of the microcosm.[4]

---

[4] Sufis of later centuries have always looked at these two ways of viewing the reality of man as essentially the same. The following is a quotation from Jāmī, the well-known

Rūmī also, although living after Ibn 'Arabī, follows the earlier terminology in his writings. Discussing the true nature of man, Rūmī remarks that philosophers say that man is the microcosm, while theosophers or Sufis say that man is the macrocosm,

The Prophet Muhammad in the company of the angels

Sufi poet of the fifteenth century, who was a continuator of Ibn 'Arabī's school and who at the same time quotes Rūmī extensively, especially in his prose doctrinal works. The first three lines of poetry are by 'Alī and show that the formulated doctrine of the macrocosm and the microcosm was known from the beginning of Islam:

"The Commander of the Faithful ('Alī) said,

"'Thy remedy is within thyself, but thou perceivest not; thy malady is from thyself, but thou seest not—

"'Thou takest thyself to be a small body, but within thee unfolds the macrocosm,

"'And thou art the Evident Book (*al kitāb al-mubīn*) through whose letters the Hidden (*al-mudmar*) becomes manifest.'

*the reason being that philosophy is confined to the phenom-
enal form of man, whereas theosophy is connected with the
essential truth of his true nature (IV, p. 301).*

*Man is in appearance a derivative of this world, and in-
trinsically the origin of the world (IV, 3767).*

*Externally the branch is the origin of the fruit; intrinsi-
cally the branch came into existence for the sake of the fruit.*

*If there had not been desire and hope of the fruit, how
should the gardener have planted the root of the tree?*

*Therefore in reality the tree was born of the fruit, (even)
if in appearance it (the fruit) was generated by the tree.*

*Hence Mustafā (Muhammad) said, "Adam and the (oth-
er) prophets are (following) behind me under (my) banner."*

*For this reason that master of (all) sorts of knowledge
[Muhammad] has uttered the allegorical saying "We are the
last and the foremost."*

*(That is to say), "If in appearance I am born of Adam, in
reality I am the forefather of (every) forefather,...*

*Therefore in reality the father (Adam) was born of me,
therefore in reality the tree was born of the fruit."*

*The thought (idea), which is first, comes last into actuality,
in particular the thought that is eternal (IV, 522 ff.).*

*So it is realized that Muhammad was the foundation [of
the Universe]. "But for thee [Muhammad] I would not have
created the heavens."[5] Every thing that exists, honor and hu-
mility, authority and high degree, all are of his dispensa-
tion and his shadow, for all have become manifest from him*
(Discourses, *p. 117*).

"(In the same vein Rūmī says:) 'If you are born of Adam, sit like him and behold all the atoms (of the Universe [reading, with Jāmī, *dharrāt* for *dhurriyyāt*]) in yourself.

"'What is in the jar that is not (also) in the river? What is in the house that is not (also) in the city?

"'This world is the jar and the heart is like the river; this world is the house [reading *khānah* for *ghurfah*], and the heart is the wonderful city'" (IV, 809-13).

"Here Rūmī—may God sanctify his spirit—calls the world a 'jar' and a 'house,' and the heart of Universal Man a 'river' and a 'city' In this he is pointing out that ev-erything that exists in the world is found in the human state...." *Naqd al-nusūs fī sharh naqsh al-fusūs*, edited by W. C. Chittick, Tehran, Anjuman-i Falsafah, 1977, p. 92.

[5] This is a well-known *hadīth qudsī*.

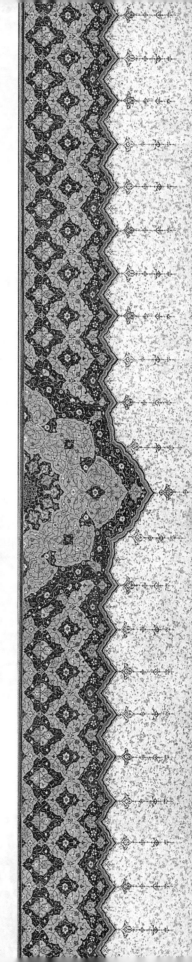

A most explicit statement of man's position in the Universe is found in the *Gulshan-i Rāz*:

Behold the world entirely contained in yourself,
That which was made last was first in thought.
The last that was made was the soul of Adam,
The two worlds were a means to his production.
There is no other final cause beyond man,
It is disclosed in man's own self....
You are a reflection of "The Adored of Angels [Adam],"
For this cause you are worshipped of angels.
Each creature that goes before you [i.e., every other
*   creature in the universe] has a soul,*
And from that soul is a cord to you.
Therefore are they all subject to your dominion,
For that the soul of each one is hidden in you.
You are the kernel of the world in the midst thereof,
Know yourself that you are the world's soul.[6]

2. The Fall

Man's state on earth as an individual cut off from his spiritual prototype is due to the fall of Adam. The fall in turn is explained by Rūmī as stemming from God's casting Iblīs (Satan) out of Heaven. According to the Quran,

We [God] created you [man]; then we shaped you,
then We said to the angels: "Bow yourselves to
Adam"; so they bowed themselves,
save Iblīs—he was not one of those that bowed themselves.
Said He, "What prevented thee to
bow thyself, when I commanded thee?"
Said he, "I am better than he; Thou
createdst me of fire, and him Thou createdst of clay."
Said He, "Get thee down out of it;
it is not for thee to wax proud here,
so go thou forth; surely thou art among the humbled"
(VII, 10-12, Arberry trans.).

[6] Vss. 261 ff.

54

شیطان لعین

angels prostrating before
n and Eve in Paradise

The reason that Iblīs did not bow down to Adam was that he saw only Adam's place in the macrocosm, i.e., only the external aspects of his nature. Moreover, Iblīs decided not to bow down to Adam through the exercise of reason, or the faculty of individual and particularized (*juz'ī*) knowledge cut off from gnosis and the illumination deriving from the Divine Intellect. See with discernment, says Rūmī,

> *Lest thou become a man blind of one eye, like Iblīs; he, like a person docked (deprived of perfect sight), sees (the one) half and not (the other) half.*
> *He saw the clay of Adam but did not see his obedience to God: he saw in him this world but did not see that (spirit) which beholds yonder world (IV, 1616–17).*

> *He (Iblīs) had knowledge, (but) since he had not religious love he beheld in Adam nothing but a figure of clay (VI, 260).*

> *He who is blessed and familiar (with spiritual mysteries) knows that intelligence [reason] is of Iblīs, while love [gnosis] is of Adam (IV, 1402).*

Iblīs is the personification of the tendency within the cosmos towards dispersion and removal from the Center, that which causes the world to separate from God. Microcosmically he personifies the tendency within man which brought about the Fall, i.e., his *nafs* or carnal self. In a similar manner the angels who bowed themselves to Adam are related to man's innermost nature and his spiritual faculties, and thus with love of God, gnosis, and integral knowledge of man's essence.

> *Forasmuch as the Angel is one in origin with Intelligence [gnosis, not reason] (and) they have (only) become two (different) forms for the sake of (the Divine) Wisdom….*
> *The Flesh (nafs) and the Devil have (also) been (essentially) one from the first, and have been an enemy and envier of Adam.*
> *He that regarded Adam as a body fled (from him in disdain) while he that regarded (him as) the trusty Light bowed (in worship) (III, 3192 ff.).*

Adam and Eve

> *The fleshly soul and the Devil both have (ever) been one person (essentially); (but) they have manifested themselves in two forms....*
>
> *You have such an enemy as this in your inward part: he is the preventer of the intellect, and the adversary of the spirit and of religion (III, 4053 ff.).*

Just as Iblīs could see nothing but externals, so was Adam's fall caused when he looked only on the external form of creation and saw the world as an independent reality cut off from God. The fall of man is the result of the blinding of the "eye of the heart" (*chashm-i dil* or *'ayn al-qalb*), which alone sees with the vision of gnosis.

> *Sick, surely, and ill-savored is the heart that knows not (cannot distinguish) the taste of this and that.*
>
> *When the heart becomes whole (is healed) of pain and disease, it will recognize the flavor of falsehood and truth [since "God taught Adam the Names"].*
>
> *When Adam's greed for the wheat [the forbidden fruit] waxed great, it robbed Adam's heart of health....*
>
> *...discernment flees from one that is drunken with vain desire (II, 2737 ff.).*

The descent of Adam to Earth

(God said), "O Adam, seek My heart-enthralling Reality: take leave of the husk and (outward) form of the (forbidden) wheat (VI, 3710).

As Frithjof Schuon has pointed out,[7] the world in Adam's original state was not yet materialized. All beings were "contemplative states" within Adam, modes of consciousness illumined with the Divine Light. Adam saw "things" as aspects of God, with no separate existence. But through "vain desire"—the sin of inquisitiveness[8]—he wanted to see things as they existed in and for themselves. Iblīs (the personification of the tendency within man towards ignorance and dispersion) tempted him to look at the state of contingent existence from the point of view of contingency itself, and as a result Adam and the whole world with him fell into that state. The direct link with God had been broken and the world was now external to Adam instead of internal.

Before the fall all creatures were bound together in harmony, manifesting the qualities of God in simultaneous richness. "Sheep and wolves lived together in peace." But with the loss of Eden, oppositions became materialized and creature was set against creature. "Get ye all down," says God in the Quran, "each of you an enemy to each" (VII, 23). An analogous sequence of events would occur if the conflicting thoughts in people's minds were suddenly to become materialized, and having become so, they were to begin to tear each other to pieces.[9]

From the moral point of view the events which brought about Adam's fall are looked upon as a sin and a shortcoming, but from a strictly metaphysical point of view it is not necessary to do so; the fall can be viewed as a necessary consequence of the unfolding of the principial possibilities or archetypes

---

[7] *Light on the Ancient Worlds*, pp. 43-47.
[8] Schuon quotes two sayings of the Prophet in this connection: "I seek refuge with God in the face of a science which is of no use to me" and "One of the claims to nobility of a Moslem rests on not paying attention to what is not his concern." *Ibid.*, p. 56.
[9] *Ibid.*, p. 47.

contained in the "Hidden Treasure." If Adam had not fallen, all of the possibilities present in the Divine Essence could not be played out. Rūmī shows something of this perspective in the following passage:

> *One mark of Adam from eternity was this, that the angels should lay their heads (on the ground) before him, because it was his place (i.e., proper to his dignity).*
>
> *Another mark was that Iblīs, saying "I am the king and the chief," should not lay down his head.*
>
> *But if Iblīs too had become a worshipper (of Adam), he (Adam) would not have been Adam: he would have been another.*
>
> *At once the worship of every angel is the test of him, and the denial (of him) by that enemy (Iblīs) is the proof of him (II, 2119-22).*

If Iblīs had not refused to bow down to Adam, this would have meant that he saw Adam's true nature, or that he saw "with both eyes." But Iblīs is precisely the personification of the tendency within the manifested universe towards separation and distance from God, and as a result he cannot see the inward nature of things. Iblīs denied Adam because this tendency towards separation and spiritual blindness does in fact exist within the universe. It is a tendency, moreover, which could not but derive from certain Names and Qualities of God: it corresponds to the possibility necessitated by the Divine Infinity that God can "negate" Himself by creating the world. Moreover, since Adam reflects all of the Divine Names and Qualities, this tendency had to exist within him also. This is why the individual self or ego is by nature far from God and unable to see the spiritual reality of things.

The separative and "negative" tendency personified by Iblīs, which is manifested on the microcosmic level by fallen man's separation from God and all of the evils which follow as a result, possesses also a positive aspect, which is particularly apparent on the level of the macrocosm. In the absence of this tendency the universe could not hold together for an instant, nor could any created being exist, for this tendency is itself

one of the constituent elements of existence. It is separation from God which "solidifies" the world.[10]

Thus if all men were to attain the state of Universal Man (which at the present state of cosmic existence is in effect an impossibility), the world would be reintegrated into the Principle, and Eden would be reestablished, i.e., the world as such would cease to exist.

In the *Mathnawī* Rūmī expresses these points by saying that heedlessness—forgetfulness of God—maintains the world: ʿĀʾishah (one of the Prophet's wives) asks the Prophet what was the true reason for the rain that had just fallen. The Prophet answers that

> ... *"this (rain) was for the purpose of allaying the grief that is upon the race of Adam in calamity [since it has lost Eden].*
> *If man were to remain in that fire of grief...*
> *... (all) selfish desires would go forth from men."*
> *Forgetfulness (of God), O beloved, is the pillar (prop) of this world; (spiritual) intelligence is a bane to this world.*
> *Intelligence belongs to that (other) world, and when it prevails, this world is overthrown.*
> *Intelligence is the sun and cupidity the ice; intelligence is the water and this world the dirt.*

---

[10] On this point see Schuon, *Transcendent Unity of Religions*, pp. 63 ff.

A little trickle (of intelligence) is coming from yonder world, that cupidity and envy may not roar (too loudly) in this world.

If the trickle from the Unseen should become greater [and intelligence is funneled into the world through those who have realized the state of Universal Man], in this world neither virtue nor vice will be left [just as the fall involved gaining the knowledge of good and evil, so regaining Paradise means going beyond good and evil] (I, 2063 ff.).

In another passage Rūmī says that he cannot reveal the divine mysteries lest

the life and livelihood (of mortals) be destroyed.

And lest the veil of forgetfulness should be entirely rent and (the meat in) the pot of tribulation be left half-raw (VI, 3527-28).

The "pot of tribulation" refers essentially to the unfolding of the principal possibilities, a point which is brought out in the following passage:

We [God] are the Revealer of the mystery, and Our work is just this, that We bring forth these hidden things [i.e., the "Hidden Treasure"] from concealment [from latency in God].

Although the thief is mute in denial (of his theft), the magistrate brings it to light by torture.

These (diverse) earths have stolen (Our) favors, so that through affliction We may bring them to confess (IV, 1014-16).

In the final analysis, the maintenance of the world depends on a balance between the contemplative who has realized the state of Universal Man, and fallen man, who lives in a state of forgetfulness. Were all men to become Universal Man, the world would vanish. Were all fallen, it would disintegrate into chaos. Each is necessary so that the principial possibilities inherent in the Divine Names and Qualities may become manifest.

Now this world goes on by reason of heedlessness; if it were not for heedlessness, this world would not remain in being. Yearning for God, recollection of the world to come, intoxication, ecstasy—these are the architects of the other world. If all these should supervene, we would to a man depart to the other world and would not remain here. God most High desires that we should be here, so that there may be two worlds. So He has appointed two sheriffs, one heedfulness and the other heedlessness, that both houses may remain inhabited (Discourses, p. 120).

3. The Trust

Just as Universal Man knows all things as they exist in God (*al-ʿārif billāh*) and not as they exist in themselves, so God knows the manifested universe as a distinctive and differentiated reality through Universal Man. In him the purpose of creation is realized: God knows the "Hidden Treasure" distinctively and multiplicity returns to unity. Rūmī expresses this by saying that God contemplates "the world of the six directions" only through Universal Man:

The owner of the Heart [Universal Man] becomes a six-faced mirror: through him God looks upon (all) the six directions.

Whosoever hath his dwelling place in (the world of) the six directions, God doth not look upon him except through the mediation of him (the owner of the Heart)....

Without him God does not bestow bounty on any one (V, 874 ff.).

Ibn ʿArabī has a similar passage: Universal Man

is to the Absolute as the pupil of the eye to the eye, through which vision takes place.... Through him God looks at His creatures and bestows mercy upon them.[11]

Universal Man, as the principle of all manifestation, is the distributor of God's bounty to the world. Thus the outward

---

[11] *Fuṣūs al-hikam*, p. 50; also translated by Izutsu, *Comparative Study*, p. 218.

harmony of the universe depends on man's collective actualization of the state of Universal Man. When a man realizes this original and primordial state, he becomes a "channel of grace" for the world. But through the fall, the majority of men have forgotten their rightful function, and thus the world becomes ever more "separated" from God and ever more chaotic.

This original function of man to be the Universal Man and act as a channel of grace for the world is referred to by the Quran as the "trust" (*al-amānah*) placed upon man's shoulders at his creation. Rūmī emphasizes the extreme importance which Sufism gives to this concept:

> *There is one thing in this world which must never be forgotten. If you were to forget everything else, but did not forget that, then there would be no cause to worry; whereas if you performed and remembered and did not forget every single thing, but forgot that one thing, then you would have done nothing whatsoever.... So man has come into this world for*

a particular task, and that is his purpose; if he does not perform it, then he will have done nothing.

> "We offered the trust to the heavens and the earth and the mountains, but they refused to carry it and were afraid of it; and man carried it. Surely he is sinful, very foolish" (Quran, XXXIII, 72).

> "We offered that trust to the heavens, but they were unable to accept it." Consider how many tasks are performed by the heavens, whereat the human reason is bewildered.... All these things they do, yet that one thing is not performed by them; that task is performed by man.

> "And We honored the Children of Adam" (Quran, XVII, 72).

> God did not say, "And We honored heaven and earth." So that task which is not performed by the heavens and the earth and the mountains is performed by man. When he performs that task, "sinfulness" and "folly" are banished from him.

> If you say, "Even if I do not perform that task, yet so many tasks are performed by me," you were not created for those other tasks. It is as though you were to procure a sword of priceless Indian steel [i.e., man's inward nature] ... and were to convert it into a butcher's knife for cutting up putrid meat, saying, "I am not letting this sword stand idle, I am putting it to so many useful purposes." ... Or it is as though you were to take a dagger of the finest temper and make of it a nail for a broken gourd (Discourses, pp. 26–27).

From the point of view of Sufism the purpose of all religion is that through the means that it provides, man may be enabled to fulfill the trust which God has placed upon his shoulders. The mission of the prophets and saints is to remind man of his original nature and to show him the way through which it may once again be actualized.

> In the composition of man all sciences were originally commingled, so that his spirit might show forth all hidden things, as limpid water shows forth all that is under it—

64

pebbles, broken shards, and the like—and all that is above it, reflecting in the substance of the water. Such is its nature, without treatment or training. But when it was mingled with earth or other colors [when Adam fell], that property and that knowledge was parted from it and forgotten by it. Then God most High sent forth prophets and saints, like a great, limpid water such as delivers out of darkness and accidental coloration every mean and dark water that enters into it. Then it remembers; when the soul of man sees itself unsullied, it knows for sure that so it was in the beginning, pure, and it knows that those shadows and colors were mere accidents (Discourses, *pp. 44-45).*

IV

Operative Sufism

Page from a manuscript of Rūmī's *Mathnawī*

IV. Operative Sufism

1. Union with God

Generally speaking, the realization by man of his primordial state—that of Universal Man in its fullness—is called from the point of view of the spiritual traveler or the "operative" (*'amalī*) aspects of the Path "union with God" (*al-wiṣāl bi'l-ḥaqq*). The path leading to union is long and difficult and has been described in a variety of ways by different Sufis. For our purposes here it is sufficient to limit ourselves to a consideration of two main steps on the Path; steps which are an application of the *Shahādah* to the spiritual travail. The first of these is *fanā'*, "annihilation of self," which derives from the "no" of the *Shahādah*: "There is *no* god but God," there is *no* reality but the Reality. Man's self-existence is not real, since he is not God; therefore the illusion that it is real must be annihilated. The second is *baqā'*, "subsistence in God," which springs from the "but": There is no reality *but* the Reality. Since God alone is real, man's real Self is God. Man attains to Reality only by passing away from his illusory self and subsiding in his real Self.

Rūmī summarizes the relationship of the *Shahādah* to the states of *fanā'* and *baqā'* as follows:

> *"Everything is perishing but His face": unless thou art in His face (essence), do not seek to exist.*
>
> *When any one has passed away (from himself) in my [God's] face, the words "everything is perishing" are not applicable (to him).*
>
> *Because he is in "but," he has transcended "no", whoever is in "but" has not passed away [in respect of his real Self] (I, 3052-54).*
>
> *When a man's "I" is negated (and eliminated) from existence, then what else remains? Consider, O denier.*

If you have an eye, open it and look! After "no," why, what else remains? (VI, 2096-97).[1]

"Die before ye die" is a Tradition of the Prophet which Rūmī often comments upon, as for example, the following:

O you who possess sincerity, (if) you want that (Reality) unveiled, choose death and tear off the veil [of your self-existence]—
Not such a death that you will go into the grave, (but) a death consisting of (spiritual) transformation (VI, 738-39).

Man should not waste his efforts in trivialities but should concentrate all of his attention on the Path, for "except dying, no other skill avails with God" (VI, 3838). The individual self is a prison which keeps man separated from God: "To be nigh (unto God) is not to go up or down: to be nigh unto God is to escape from the prison of existence" (III, 4514). For this reason, the seekers of God

desire that friendship and passion and love and unbelief and faith may no more remain, so that they may rejoin their origin. For these things are all walls and a cause of narrowness and duality. (Discourses, p. 203).

All such individual attributes must be transcended, for they pertain only to self-existence.

Do not say that the heart that is bound (conditioned) by (such bodily attributes as) sadness and laughter is worthy of seeing Thee....
He who is bound by sadness and laughter is living by means of these two borrowed (transient and unreal) things.
In the verdant garden of Love, which is without end, there are many fruits besides sorrow and joy.
Love is higher than these two states of feeling: without spring and without autumn it is (ever) green and fresh (I, 1791-94).

[1] Nicholson's translation of these two passages from the *Mathnawī* has been slightly modified ("no" for "not" and "but" for "except") to show more clearly the relevance to the present discussion.

It is love, in fact, which is the means whereby man dies to self, for "Love is an attribute of God" (V, 2185) which burns up "the attributes of self, hair by hair" (III, 1922). When love—which as explained earlier implies the realized aspect of knowledge and the attachment of man to God—becomes truly actualized, the limitations of the individual self are surpassed.

> *Thou art a lover of God, and God is such that when He comes there is not a single hair of thee (remaining).*
>
> *At that look (of His) a hundred like thee vanish away....*
>
> *Thou art a shadow [i.e., composed of nothing but the limitations of the ego[2]] and in love with the sun: the sun comes, the shadow is naughted speedily (III, 4621-23).*

> *Such a non-existent one who has gone from himself (become selfless) is the best of beings and the great (one among them [men]).*
>
> *...In passing away he really hath the life everlasting.*
>
> *All spirits are under his governance; all bodies too are in his control [since he is Universal Man] (IV, 398-400).*

> *The higher any one goes [on the ladder of attachment to the ego], the more foolish he is, for his bones will be worse broken.*

[2] "The Divine Love is the Sun of perfection: the (Divine) Word is its light, the creatures are as shadows" (VI, 983).

This is (constitutes) the derivatives (of the subject), and its fundamental principles are that to exalt one's self is (to claim) co-partnership with God.

Unless thou hast died and become living through Him, thou art an enemy seeking to reign in co-partnership (with Him).

When thou hast become living through Him, that (which thou hast become) is in sooth He; it is absolute Unity; how is it co-partnership?

Seek the explanation of this in the mirror of devotional works, for thou wilt not gain the understanding of it from speech and discourse (IV, 2764-68).

> Love came, and went again,
> Like blood within my flesh and vein;
> From self Love set me free
> And with the Friend completed me.
>
> Only remains my name;
> My being's every particle
> The Friend took for His claim,
> And so the Friend became my whole (Rubā'īyāt, *p. 45*).
>
> Since first I heard men cry
> The famous tale of Love,
> With heart and soul and eye
> In its cause I strove.
>
> "Perchance," I said, "the Loved,
> And he that loves, are twain":
> But lo, the twain one proved,
> My sight it was, was vain (Rubā'īyāt, *p. 48*).

Union with God is complete absorption in Him, such that

the one absorbed is no longer there; he can make no more effort; he ceases to act and to move; he is immersed in the water. Any action that proceeds from him is not his action, it is the action of the water. (Discourses, *p. 55*).

> Dost thou suppose
> I do as I command,

Or, as the moment goes,
I am in my own hand?

As a pen I lie
Before my scrivener,
Or like a ball am I,
*My mallet's prisoner (*Rubāʿīyāt, *p. 17)*

Rūmī (on his mule) meets Shams-i Tabrīzī for the first time

When an attempt is made to define the state of union closely, the most that can be done is to divest it of all the limitations which condition existence. Such limitations have only a sort of "negative reality," whereas in the state of union only positive reality, i.e., God, remains.[3]

> *What is to be done, O Moslems? for I do not recognize*
> *myself.*
> *I am neither Christian, nor Jew, nor Gabr, nor Moslem.*
> *I am not of the East, nor of the West, nor of the land, nor*
> *of the sea;*
> *I am not of nature's mint, nor of the circling heavens.*
> *I am not of earth, nor of water, nor of air, nor of fire;*
> *I am not of the empyrean, nor of the dust, nor of existence,*
> *nor of entity.*
> *I am not of India, nor of China, nor of Bulgaria, nor of*
> *Saqsīn;*
> *I am not of the kingdom of 'Irāqain, nor of the country of*
> *Khorāsān.*
> *I am not of this world, nor of the next, nor of Paradise,*
> *nor of Hell;*
> *I am not of Adam, nor of Eve, nor of Eden and Rizwān.*
> *My place is the Placeless, my trace is the Traceless;[4]*
> *'Tis neither body nor soul, for I belong to the soul of the*
> *Beloved.*
> *I have put duality away, I have seen that the two worlds*
> *are one;*
> *One I seek, One I know, One I see, One I call….*
> *I am intoxicated with Love's cup, the two worlds have*
> *passed out of my ken….*
> *…I am so drunken in this world,*
> *That except of drunkenness and revelry I have no tale to*
> *tell (Dīwān, pp. 125-27).[5]*

[3] See Guénon, "Oriental Metaphysics," p. 12.

[4] "You are of where, (but) your origin is in Nowhere." (II, 612). "If he that is 'born of the Spirit' is like the wind of which thou 'canst not tell whence it cometh, and whither it goeth,' this is because, being identified with the Self, he is without origin; he has come forth from the chain of cosmic causation and dwells in the Changeless." Schuon, *Gnosis: Divine Wisdom*, p. 85.

[5] This poem is not included in the critical edition of the *Dīwān* by Furūzānfar (which appeared many years after Nicholson's book), though it is found in some manuscripts

Scholars of religion have often come to the conclusion that union with God or deliverance as expounded in oriental doctrines is complete extinction such that the individual is "a drop of water in the sea" and thus loses all that he ever was. In some respects this is true, as is witnessed by many of Rūmī's formulations. But if the individual loses that which he was, he only loses what in itself is privation and nothingness. Union implies nothing negative; according to all traditional doctrines its real nature is absolute plenitude.[6] If the goal is presented in negative terms, it is because in relation to the world God is "nothing," but this is only because the world is nothing in relation to God. And it is God who is real, not the world.

The basic question to be asked when considering the doctrine of union is "What is man's real self?" In his *Risālat al-*

and uncritical editions, and it is from these that Nicholson must have taken it. Although it is probably spurious, it does represent Rumi's perspective.
[6] See Guénon, "Oriental Metaphysics," p. 12.

ahadiyyah, Ibn 'Arabī says, "He sent Himself with Himself to Himself."[7] Through the spiritual path man awakens from his slumber and finds that he is not what he had thought himself to be; he is not that particular mode of consciousness with which he had identified himself. And man does not "achieve" anything by realizing union with God; rather he becomes what he had always been in his inmost nature.[8] God is the Real and nothing can be outside of His Reality.

> *Take the famous utterance "I am God."[9] Some men reckon it a great pretension; but "I am God" is in fact a great humility. The man who says "I am the servant of God" asserts that two exist, one himself and the other God. But he who says "I am God" has naughted himself and cast himself to the winds. He says, "I am God": that is, "I am not, He is all, nothing has existence but God, I am pure nonentity, I am nothing." In this the humility is greater* (Discourses, *pp. 55-56*).

2. The Nafs

A theme to which Rūmī often returns is that the ego or carnal self (*nafs*)[10] is a veil which prevents man from knowing his own true nature.

> *We have been in heaven, we have been friends of the angels;*
> *Thither, sire, let us return, for that is our country* (Dīwān,
> *p. 33*).

---

[7] Quoted in Nasr, *Three Muslim Sages*, p. 107.

[8] "'No man hath ascended up to heaven, but he that came down from heaven.' To 'ascend up to heaven' is to 'become One-self,' that is to say, to become that which one had never really ceased to be, in the sense that the essence of the ego is the Self, that 'Life' which we can only purchase by losing the life of 'me.'" Schuon, *Gnosis: Divine Wisdom*, p. 85.

[9] Or "I am the Truth." The reference is to al-Hallāj.

[10] It is of course true that the concept of the "*nafs*" in Sufism is much more complicated than what might be indicated by the present discussion. For example, in section 3 below it is pointed out that the individual self must be transformed on the spiritual path. This transformation is often described in terms of the three stages of the *nafs* according to the Quranic terminology: the *nafs-i ammārah* ("the soul which incites" to evil) with which we are essentially concerned here, the *nafs-i lawwāmah* ("the soul which reproaches" itself for its own shortcomings), and the *nafs-i mutma'innah* ("the soul at peace" with God).

O thou who hast a country
Beyond the skies,
Yet didst of earth and ashes
Thyself surmise:

Thou hast engraved thine image
Upon the earth,
Forgetting that far country
Which gave thee birth
(Rubā'īyāt, *p. 8*).

Mawlānā performing the dance of remembrence

Man's original food is the Light of God: animal food is
improper for him;
But, in consequence of disease, his mind has fallen into
this (delusion), that day and night he should eat of water
and clay (III, 1083-84).

O how long shall we, like children in the earthly sphere
Fill our lap with dust and stones and shards?
Let us give up the earth and fly heavenwards,
Let us flee from childhood to the banquet of men.
Behold how the earthly frame has entrapped thee!
Rend the sack and raise thy head clear (Dīwān, p. 119).

Give up this (belief in phenomena). Loves (felt) for what
is endued with form have not as their object the form or the
lady's face. . . .
The sunbeam shone on the wall: the wall received a borrowed splendor.
Why set your heart on a piece of turf, O simple man? Seek
out the source which shines perpetually (II, 702, 708-9).

You are an idol-worshipper when you remain in (bondage to) forms: leave its (the idol's) form and look at the reality (I, 2893).

The cardinal sin in Islam is the association (*shirk*) of other divinities with God or "polytheism." As indicated above, "There is no god," the negative half of the *Shahādah* (*nafy*), implies the non-existence of all that is other than God. Sufism applies the *Shahādah* with its full force and in the light of its profoundest meaning and therefore says that to believe that any phenomenon whatever exists independently of God is to associate that phenomenon with Him. The true "monotheist" (*muwaḥḥid*) sees with the vision of gnosis that all things depend absolutely upon God and derive their total reality from Him. The "associator" or polytheist (*mushrik*), however, suffers from an optical illusion whose source is his attribution of reality to his own individual self. As long as he has not escaped from the limitations of his ego he cannot help but act as if phenomena were independent realities, detached from God.

> *Throw dust on your sense-perceiving eye: the sensuous eye is the enemy of intellect and religion.*
> *God has called the sensuous eye blind [cf. Quran, VII, 178]; He has said that it is an idolater and our foe,*
> *Because it saw the foam and not the sea, because it saw the present and not tomorrow (II, 1607-9).*

> *The idol of your self is the mother of (all) idols...(I, 772).*

> *If ye pass beyond form, O friends, 'tis Paradise and rose-gardens within rose-gardens.*
> *When thou hast broken and destroyed thine own form, thou hast learned to break the form of everything (III, 578-79).*

The remedy for association or polytheism is death to self, a death which comes about when man is effaced by love, but a love which, as we have already noted, is in essence the vision of gnosis and the realization that God alone is real.

> *... Hail, O mighty Love, destroyer of polytheism!*

Verily He is the First and the Last: do not regard polytheism as arising from aught except the eye that sees double [because of self-existence] (V, 590-91).

Just as existence in and for the individual self necessitates that man be separated from God in this world, so also does it necessitate separation in the next world, and this in the view of Sufism is one of the profound implications of the concept of "hell." As long as man remains attached to what is transitory—the ego and the world—he is far from God.

> *Therefore union with this (world) is separation from that (world): the health of this body is the sickness of the spirit.*
>
> *Hard is the separation from this transitory abode: know, then, that the separation from that permanent abode is harder.*
>
> *Since it is hard for thee to be separated from the form, how hard must it be to be parted from its Maker!*
>
> *O thou that hast not the patience to do without the vile world, how, O friend, how hast thou the patience to do without God?…*
>
> *Take heed, never be wedded to self (IV, 3209-12, 3219).*

> *That captain of mankind [the Prophet] has said truly that no one who has passed away from this world*
>
> *Feels sorrow and regret and disappointment on account of death; nay, but he feels a hundred regrets for having missed the opportunity,*
>
> *Saying (to himself), "Why did not I make death my object—(death which is) the storehouse of every fortune and every provision—*
>
> *(And why), through seeing double, did I make the lifelong object of my attention those phantoms that vanished at the fated hour?"*
>
> *The grief of the dead is not on account of death; it is because (so they say) "We dwelt upon the (phenomenal) forms,*
>
> *And this we did not perceive, that those are (mere) form and foam, (and that) the foam is moved and fed by the Sea" (VI, 1450-55).*

Before his fall man reflected integrally and consciously the divine Reality—"God created Adam in His Own image"[11]—and thus contained within himself the principle of all Existence, with which he was in perfect equilibrium. But through his fall he lost his inward contact with God, and for him the equilibrium of the universe became blurred. Trying to regain his original state man created his own equilibrium and saw things not as they are—in God—but through the veil of his individual self. The process of death, whether in the sense of the Prophet's words, "Die before ye die," or in the usual physical sense, implies precisely a return to, or at least a renewed awareness of, man's original equilibrium with the universe.

If at death a man "goes to hell" it is because of his own nature: he has created in himself an artificial equilibrium and set himself up as the standard of measurement, whereas "man is the measure of all things" only if he sees in and through God, for there is no other absolute standard. The Prophet said, "Man is asleep and when he dies he awakens": man comes to see existence as it is and not as he thinks it is. If his being does not conform to the equilibrium of the universe, he is separated from his proper place in "God's Order," and the equilibrium of the universe appears to him as a chaos. His point of reference and standard of measurement is still his own ego. "Oh, there is many a raw (imperfect) one," says Rūmī

whose blood was shed externally, but whose living fleshly soul escaped to yonder side.

[11] This is a well-known *hadīth* of the Prophet.

Its instrument was shattered, but the brigand was left alive: the fleshly soul is living though that on which it rode has bled to death (V, 3822-23).

Make it thy habit to behold the Light without the glass [the intermediaries of phenomenal forms and the self], in order that when the glass is shattered there may not be blindness (in thee) (V, 991).

It is the individual self which separates man from God, and ultimately, "This carnal self (*nafs*) is Hell...." (I, 1375); to put out the fires of hell a man must pass away from self:

(Inasmuch as) ye have answered the call of God and have brought water [the "water of life"—love] into the blazing hell of your soul—

Our [God's] Hell also in regard to you has become greenery and roses and plenty and riches (II, 2567-68).

Hell exists for man only when the carnal soul "escapes to yonder side":

Everyone's death is the same quality as himself, my lad: to the enemy (of God) an enemy, and to the friend of God a friend....

Your fear of death in fleeing (from it) is (really) your fear of yourself. Take heed, O (dear) soul!

'Tis your (own) ugly face, not the visage of Death: your spirit is like the tree, and death (is like) the leaf.

It has grown from you, whether it is good or evil: every hidden thought of yours, foul or fair, is (born) from yourself.

If you are wounded by a thorn, you yourself have sown;

Shams-i Tabrīzī foretells his own death to Rūmī

and if you are (clad) in satin and silk, you yourself have spun (III, 3489 sqq.).

3. Knowledge and Method

The heart, the center of man's being, is identified in its innermost nature with man's archetypes or principal possibilities; it links him directly to the world of the Spirit.

I said to my heart, "How is it
My heart, that in foolishness
You are barred from the service
Of Him whose name you bless?"

My heart replied, "You do wrong
To misread me in this way,
I am constant in His service,
You are the one astray" (Discourses, *p. 178*).

Rūmī often refers to the following *hadīth qudsī*: "Neither My earth nor My heavens contain Me, but I am contained in the heart of My faithful servant." In the following passages he comments on this theme:

I gazed into my own heart;
There I saw Him; He was nowhere else (Dīwān, *p. 73*).

O heart, we have searched from end to end: I saw in thee naught save the Beloved.
Call me not infidel, O heart, if I say, "Thou thyself art He" (Dīwān, *p. 250*).

Here the understanding becomes silent or (else) it leads into error, because the heart is with Him, or indeed the heart is He (I, 3489).

To know the heart in its inmost essence is to know God, and to the degree that one truly knows God, one is not other than He, for a being defined by relativity cannot know the Absolute. To know God,

one must "become" God, by ceasing to exist in that mode of being which separates man from Him, or by no longer being defined by the limitations of that state.

> When the spirit became lost in contemplation, it said this:
> "None but God has contemplated the beauty of God" (Dīwān, p. 91).
>
> Do not look on that Beauteous One with your own eye: behold the Sought with the eye of seekers.
> Shut your own eye to that sweet-eyed One; borrow an eye from His lovers.
> Nay, borrow eye and sight from Him, then look on His face with His eye (IV, 75-77).

> *When your essence is pure from all stain....*
> *There remains no distinction,*
> *Knower and Known are one and the same.*[12]

Intelligence in the true sense, which is a faculty centered in the heart and not in the mind, exists in man to discriminate between the Real and the unreal.[13] But the ego-centric illusion, the *nafs* and its concomitants, stands between man and true knowledge. As a result man constantly mistakes the illusory projection of things within himself for things as they are in reality. True intelligence is to see things as they are through God; and to see things through God, one cannot be other than He.

The only value of external knowledge as such is its symbolical effectiveness, or the extent to which it can lead to the inward reality of that which it manifests outwardly.

> *The (right) thought is that which opens a way: the (right) way*
> *is that on which a (spiritual) king advances (II, 3207).*

Every expression of the truth is in a sense relative since it exists in the world of forms and relativity, but in another sense it is absolute, for it is a symbol reflecting the ultimate Truth itself, which alone is absolute "in the absolute sense."[14] This is why Sufism, in spite of its constant emphasis upon "breaking forms," stresses the importance of orthodoxy:[15] only if a doctrine or method is orthodox, or in other words, only if on its own level it is an adequate reflection of Truth, can it lead to the Truth. For someone to alter the doctrine in terms of his own personal opinion (*zann*) is to destroy its value as a symbol and therefore its ability to reflect the Truth. In some respects this explains the function of the spiritual master —since in his inner being he has transcended the world of forms and lives in the world of the Spirit, he can reformulate the doctrine

---

[12] *Gulshan-i Rāz*, verses 412-13.

[13] See Schuon, *"Religio Perennis,"* in *Light on the Ancient Worlds*, chapter 9.

[14] This is not a redundancy. Schuon has pointed out the importance of the concept of the "relatively absolute" in a number of his writings. See for example *Transcendent Unity of Religions*, pp. 110-11 and *Stations of Wisdom*, pp. 27-28.

[15] Far from being synonymous with sterility and dull conformity, orthodoxy in the traditional sense is the guarantee that a doctrine expresses the supraformal Truth on the formal plane in a manner conformable to the conditions of that plane. See Schuon, "Orthodoxy and Intellectuality," in *Stations of Wisdom*, chapter 1.

in a manner that suits the particular needs of the collectivity which he is addressing.

In the *Mathnawī* Rūmī summarizes the Sufi point of view on the importance of orthodoxy by criticizing a man who had interpreted some Traditions of the Prophet to his own advantage: "Alter yourself, not the Traditions: abuse your (dull) brain, not the rose-garden (the true sense which you cannot apprehend)" (I, 3744). Man must not bring the doctrine down

"The Tavern" often symbolizes the meeting of spiritual travelers

to his own level; rather, he must rise to its level.

In a traditional civilization all of the branches of knowledge are determined in accordance with principles deriving from the spiritual realm; if one goes deeply into them, he is led from the formal expression to the supra-formal Truth.

(In order to tread this Way) one needs a knowledge whereof the root is Yonder, inasmuch as every branch is a guide to the root (III, 1124).

Those persons who have made or are in the course of making their studies think that if they constantly attend here [i.e., if they come to Rūmī for instruction in Sufism] they will forget and abandon all that they have learned [since Sufism "does away with" formal expression]. On the contrary, when they come here their sciences all acquire a soul. For the sciences are like images; when they acquire a soul, it is as though a lifeless body has received a soul.

All knowledge has its origin beyond, transferring from the world without letters and sounds to the world of letters and sounds (Discourses, *pp. 163-64).*

As we have seen, to truly "know" a reality pertaining to the spiritual world, man must "become" it: in the worlds beyond form, knowledge and being are wed. It is the role of symbolism to indicate the way that man must follow in realizing the possibilities of existence latent in his own essence.

Each level of reality is a symbolical expression of the levels above it, since ontologically it is determined by them. For the traveler on the spiritual path, a higher state of being appears first as a vision within him, and as he progresses he is gradually absorbed into it. By the successive realization of the levels of being man can ultimately realize the state of union with the Divine itself.

> *You draw that knowledge towards yourself. It says, "I cannot be contained here, and you are tardy in arriving there. It is impossible for me to be contained here, and it is difficult for you to come there." To bring about the impossible is impossible; but to bring about the difficult is not impossible. So, though it is difficult, strive to attain the great knowledge; and do not expect that it will be contained here, for that is impossible (*Discourses, p. 216).

The spiritual method of Sufism, whereby theoretical knowledge is actualized so that it becomes part of man's being, is essentially concentration upon the Truth through coordination and realization of the inherent powers of the human state.[16] The fundamental tendency of fallen man is dispersive. Since he lives as if he were only his ego, his intelligence is "externalized" and scattered. It is "distributed over a hundred unimportant affairs, over thousands of desires and great matters and small" (IV, 3288). The immediate purpose of the method is to reverse this dispersive tendency; and since man's present condition results from "forgetfulness" (*ghaflah*) of his own pretemporal essence, the means through which concentration is brought about is known as *dhikr*, "remembrance" of God.

Just as in common Arabic usage the word *dhikr* also means "to call upon," so in its technical Sufi meaning "to remember God" also means "to call upon God," and the central method

---

[16] On concentration in Sufism see Burckhardt, *Introduction to Sufi Doctrine*, pp. 112 ff. and Nasr, "Sufism and the Integration of Man," in *Sufi Essays*, chapter 2.

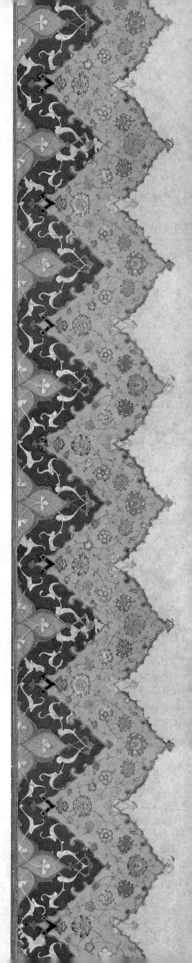

of the Path is the invocation of the divine Name, the Name which is mysteriously identical with the Named, for it is its perfect symbol.

Various formulas and divine Names are employed in Sufi invocation. In what is usually known as invocation of the "Supreme Name" (*ism-i a'zam*) the Name invoked is viewed as containing within itself all of the Names of God: it is a means of realizing all of the states of being contained in man's essence, or of actualizing all of the names which "God taught Adam." Through the invocation man is reintegrated into his center and ultimately attains union with God.

As mentioned above the heart itself is never apart from God; it is man's individual self that through the spiritual method must be transformed in order for man to reassume his rightful place in the Universe.

> *Hence it is realized that the heart in all circumstances is attached to the heart's beloved, and has no need to traverse the stages [of the Path], no need to fear highwaymen [hindrances on the way].... It is the wretched body which is fettered to these things* (Discourses, *pp. 177-78).*

In Sufism "spiritual virtue"[17] is the reflection in the human and social spheres of the spiritual transformation undergone on the path. It is the equilibrium of the innermost faculties of the soul brought about by the reintegration of man into his center and reflected outwardly in the participation of man's mental and psycho-physical dimensions in the Truth. A truly "virtuous" man is thus one whose whole being, including the body, has become a mirror reflecting God.[18] Moreover, virtue is in no way "something of merit," for it does not belong to the human being as an individual. It is the "natural" state of man before his fall, a state which is attained through the removal from man of all that which is opaque and prevents the radiation of the divine Light.

[17] On spiritual virtue see Schuon, *Spiritual Perspectives and Human Facts*, London, 1954, Part IV; Burckhardt, *Introduction to Sufi Doctrine*, pp. 107-12; and Schuon, *Understanding Islam*, pp. 130-33.
[18] See *Mathnawī*, I, 34; IV, p. 508; and V, 3922.

It should not be concluded from a study of spiritual method in Sufism that the Sufis believe that all one has to do to become a saint is to enter the Path. Not all initiates reach a state of knowledge beyond forms, and very few reach the ultimate goal, or union.[19] It is perhaps true to say that the great majority of the members of a Sufi order have been, or in our days at least are, among the *mutabarrikūn*, the "blessed," those who receive passively the spiritual grace of the master and are content to practice a religious life somewhat more intense than that of their pious neighbors. Only a small number are truly *sālikūn*, "travelers" on the Path, in the sense of progressing from one spiritual state[20] to another.

Sufism stresses, moreover, that participation in its spiritual means, at whatever level this may take place—from simple initiation to the most advanced stages of the Path—, can be attained only through the grace of God and His "confirmation" of man's efforts (*ta'yīd*). The spiritual disciplines of Sufism, such as invocation and meditation[21] and such secondary means as music[22] and the sacred dance, are never considered as capable of achieving anything by themselves. They are practices which can only become effective through the grace present in their sacred forms and confirmation from on High. Would-be critics of the use of any kind of "method" to attract the divine Grace would do well to contemplate these verses of Rūmī:

> *If you say that (spiritual) purity is [only] (bestowed by) the grace of God [and not by method], [you must nevertheless realize that] this success in polishing (the heart [i.e., in practicing the disciplines of the Path]) is also (derived) from that (Divine) bounty.*

[19] All initiates who faithfully follow the disciplines of the Path do, however, in the words of Shaykh al-'Alawī, "rise high enough to have at least inward Peace." Quoted in Lings, *A Sufi Saint of the Twentieth Century*, p. 22.

[20] On the spiritual states and stations see Nasr, "The Spiritual States in Sufism," *Sufi Essays*, chapter 5.

[21] On invocation and meditation see Burckhardt, *Introduction to Sufi Doctrine*, part two, chapters 3 and 4.

[22] On the relationship of Sufism to music see Nasr, "The Influence of Sufism on Traditional Persian Music," *Studies in Comparative Religion*, vol. 6, 1972, pp. 225-34; also in *Islamic Culture*, 1971 (no. 3), pp. 171-79.

That (devotional) work and prayer is in proportion to the (worshipper's) aspirations: "Man has nothing but what he has striven after [Quran, LIII, 40]."

God alone is the giver of aspiration: no base churl aspires to be a king (IV, 2911-13).

4. The Limitations of Rational Knowledge

As we have seen, in Rūmī's view external knowledge, or knowledge in the usual sense of the term, is useful and justifiable only to the extent that it is symbolically effective. Man should never be satisfied to "know" with the feeble powers of his reason. Rather he should enter the Path in order to be delivered from the limitations of reason and attain to gnosis.

> *From God came (the text), "Verily, opinion doth not enable (you) to dispense (with the Truth) [Quran, LIII, 29]": when did the steed of opinion run (mount) to the Heavens?…*
>
> *Come, recognize that your imagination and reflection and sense-perception and apprehension are like the reed-cane on which children ride.*
>
> *The sciences of the mystics bear them (aloft); The sciences of sensual men are burdens to them.…*
>
> *God hath said, "(Like an ass) laden with his books [Quran, LXII, 5]": burdensome is the knowledge that is not from Himself.*
>
> *The knowledge that is not immediately from Himself does not endure (I, 3442 ff.).*
>
> *Blind inwardly, they [worldly men] put their heads out of the window of the physical body. What will they see? What does their approval or disapproval amount to? To the intelligent man both are one and the same; since they have seen neither to approve or*

A bull pays tribute to Mawlānā

A goldsmith's hammering causes Mawlānā to dance

disapprove, whichever they say is nonsense (*Discourses*, p. 100).

Vision is superior to knowledge: hence the present world prevails (over the next world) in the view of the vulgar,

Because they regard this world as ready money, while they deem what concerns that (other) world to be (like) a debt (III, 3858-59).

Since thou art a part of the world, howsoever thou art thou deemest all [including the saints] to be of the same description as thyself, misguided man....

(If) a cow come suddenly into Baghdad and pass from this side (of the city) to that (farther) side,

Of all (its) pleasures and joys and delights she will see nothing but the rind of a watermelon (IV, 2368, 2377-78).

The philosopher is in bondage to things perceived by the intellect [the reason]; (but) the pure (saint) is he that rides as a prince on the Intellect of intellect.

The Intellect of intellect is your kernel, (while) your intellect is (only) the husk: the belly of animals is ever seeking husks.

He that sees the kernel has a hundred loathings for the husk: to the goodly (saints) the kernel (alone) is lawful, lawful.

When the intellect, (which is) the husk, offers a hundred evidences, how should the Universal Intellect take a step without having certainty? (III, 2527-30).

Know that (true) knowledge consists in seeing fire plainly, not in prating that smoke is evidence of fire....

O you whose evidence is like a staff in your hand (which) indicates that you suffer from blindness,

(All this) noise and pompous talk and assumption of authority (only means), "I cannot see: (kindly) excuse me" (VI, 2505 ff.).

We are much addicted to subtle discussions, we are exceedingly fond of solving problems;

And to the end that we may tie knots and (then) undo them, (we are) making many rules for (posing and stating) the difficulty and for answering (the questions, raised by it).[23]

Like a bird which should undo the fastenings of a snare, and tie (them together) at times, in order that it might become perfect in skill:

It is deprived of the open country and meadowland, its life is spent in dealing with knots (II, 3733–36).

Suppose the knot is loosed, O adept (thinker): 'tis (like) a tight knot on an empty purse.

Thou hast grown old in (the occupation of) loosing knots: suppose a few more knots are loosed (by thee, what then?)

The knot that is (fastened) tight on our throat is that thou shouldst know whether thou art vile or fortunate.

Solve this problem if thou art a man: spend thy breath (life) on this, if thou hast the breath (spirit) of Adam (within thee).

Suppose thou knowest the definitions of (all) substances and accidents (how shall it profit thee?): know the (true) definition of thyself, for this is indispensable.

When thou knowest the definition of thyself, flee from this definition, that thou mayst attain to Him who hath no definition, O sifter of dust.

---

[23] "This unhealthy taste for research, real 'mental restlessness' without end and without issue, shows itself at its very plainest in modern philosophy, the greater part of which represents no more than a series of quite artificial problems, which only exist because they are badly propounded, owing their origin and survival to nothing but carefully kept up verbal confusions" R. Guénon, *East and West*, London, 1941, pp. 85-86.

> *(Thy) life has gone (to waste) in (the consideration of logical) predicate and subject: (thy) life, devoid of (spiritual) insight, has gone in (study of) what has been received by hearsay.*
>
> *Every proof (that is) without (a spiritual) result and effect is vain: consider the (final) result of thyself! (V, 560-67).*

> *The great scholars of the age split hairs on all manner of sciences. They know perfectly and have a complete comprehension of those matters which do not concern them. But as for what is truly of moment and touches a man more closely than all else, namely his own self, this your great scholar does not know* (Discourses, p. 30).

Man must know himself in order that he can escape from himself; all other knowledge is worthless. "Make a journey out of self into [your real] self, O master, / For by such a journey earth becomes a quarry of gold" (*Dīwān*, p. 111). Once a man has entered upon the spiritual Path, and has made progress upon it,

> *The illumination of the spirit comes: (then) there remains not, O thou who seekest illumination, conclusion and premise or that which contradicts (a statement or) that which renders (its acceptance) necessary.*
>
> *Because the seer on whom His (God's) Light is dawning is quite independent of the (logical) proof which resembles a (blind man's) staff (I, 1507-8).*

> *(… in the case of) that truth which is immediate and intuitive, there is no room for any interpretation (II, 3248).*

Moreover, it does a person no good to argue that he is investigating this or that branch of knowledge "for the glory of God."

> *All these sciences and exertions and acts of devotion in comparison with the majesty and merit of the Creator, are as though a man bowed to you, performed a service, and departed. If you were to set the whole world upon your heart in serving God, it would amount to the same thing as bowing your head once to the ground* (Discourses, p. 212).

Man cannot truly act according to the will of God unless he himself is not acting. "Except dying, no other skill avails with God" (VI, 3838). "The root of the root of love and fealty is to die and be naught" (V, 1253-54).

What is there that God most High does not possess and of which He is in need? [Obviously, nothing. Then] it is necessary to bring before God most High a heart mirror-bright, so that He may see His own face in it. "God looks not at your forms, nor at your deeds, but at your hearts"[24] (Discourses, p. 195).

What is the mirror of Being? Not-being. Bring not-being [death to self] (as your gift [to God]), if you are not a fool (I, 3201).

Calligraphy of the Name of the Essence (*Huwa*)

---

[24] A *hadīth* of the Prophet.

Biographical Notes

WILLIAM C. CHITTICK is a professor in the Department of Asian and Asian-American Studies at the State University of New York, Stony Brook. He is author and translator of twenty-five books and one hundred articles on Sufism, Shī'ism, and Islamic thought in general. Among his publications are *The Sufi Path of Love: The Spiritual Teachings of Rumi* (1983), *The Psalms of Islam* (1988), *The Self-Disclosure of God: Principles of Ibn al-'Arabī's Cosmology* (1998), *Sufism: A Short Introduction* (2000), *The Heart of Islamic Philosophy: The Quest for Self-Knowledge in the Teachings of Afdal al-Dīn Kāshānī* (2001), and *Me & Rumi: The Autobiography of Shams-i Tabrizi* (2004).

SEYYED HOSSEIN NASR is University Professor of Islamic Studies at the George Washington University. The author of over fifty books and five hundred articles, he is one of the world's most respected writers and speakers on Islam, its arts and sciences, and its traditional mystical path, Sufism. His publications include *Sufi Essays*, *Knowledge and the Sacred*, *Religion and the Order of Nature*, *A Young Muslim's Guide to the Modern World*, *The Heart of Islam: Enduring Values for Humanity*, and *Islam: Religion, History, and Civilization*. A volume in the prestigious *Library of Living Philosophers* series has been dedicated to his thought.

Index

For a glossary of all key foreign words used
in books published by World Wisdom, including
metaphysical terms in English, consult:
www.DictionaryofSpiritualTerms.com.
This on-line Dictionary of Spiritual Terms
provides extensive definitions, examples and related
terms in other languages.

Titles in the Spiritual Masters: East & West Series

The Essential Shinran: A Buddhist Path of True Entrusting,
edited by Alfred Bloom, 2007

The Essential Sri Anandamayi Ma: Illustrated,
by Alexander Lipski and Anandamayi Ma, 2007

The Essential Swami Ramdas: Commemorative Edition,
compiled by Susunaga Weeraperuma, 2005

Frithjof Schuon: Messenger of the Perennial Philosophy,
by Michael Oren Fitzgerald, 2010

The Golden Age of Zen: Zen Masters of the T'ang Dynasty,
by John C.H. Wu, 2003

Honen the Buddhist Saint: Essential Writings and Official Biography,
edited by Joseph A. Fitzgerald, 2006

Introduction to Hindu Dharma: Illustrated
by Jagadguru His Holiness Sri Chandrasekharendra Saraswati Swamigal,
Sankaracharya of Kanchi,
edited by Michael Oren Fitzgerald, 2008

The Laughing Buddha of Tofukuji: The Life of Zen Master Keido Fukushima,
by Ishwar C. Harris, 2004

Messenger of the Heart: The Book of Angelus Silesius,
by Frederick Franck, 2005

The Original Gospel of Ramakrishna: Based on M.'s English Text, Abridged,
revised by Swami Abhedananda,
edited and abridged by Joseph A. Fitzgerald, 2011

Paths to Transcendence: According to Shankara, Ibn Arabi, and Meister Eckhart,
by Reza Shah-Kazemi, 2006

*Samdhong Rinpoche: Uncompromising Truth for a Compromised World:
Tibetan Buddhism and Today's World*,
edited by Donovan Roebert, 2006

A Spirit of Tolerance: The Inspiring Life of Tierno Bokar,
by Amadou Hampaté Bâ, edited by Roger Gaetani, 2008

The Sufi Doctrine of Rumi: Illustrated Edition,
by William C. Chittick, 2005

Timeless in Time: Sri Ramana Maharshi,
by A. R. Natarajan, 2006